Also by Jill Conner Browne

The Sweet Potato Queens' Guide to Raising Children for Fun and Profit

The Sweet Potato Queens' First Big-Ass Novel: Stuff We Didn't Actually Do,
but Could Have, and May Yet
(with Karin Gillespie)

The Sweet Potato Queens' Wedding Planner/Divorce Guide

The Sweet Potato Queens' Field Guide to Men: Every Man I Love
Is Either Married, Gay, or Dead

The Sweet Potato Queens' Big-Ass Cookbook (and Financial Planner)

God Save the Sweet Potato Queens

The Sweet Potato Queens' Book of Love

American Thighs

The Sweet Potato Queens' Guide to Preserving Your Assets

Jill Conner Browne

SIMON & SCHUSTER   New York • London • Toronto • Sydney

Simon & Schuster
1230 Avenue of the Americas
New York, NY 10020

First Simon & Schuster hardcover edition January 2009

SIMON & SCHUSTER and colophon are registered trademarks of Simon & Schuster, Inc.

Sweet Potato Queens® is a registered trademark of Jill Conner Browne.

The Sweet Potato Queens® characters, names, titles, logos, and all related indicia are trademarks of Jill Conner Browne and/or SPQ, Inc. All trademarks, trade names, trade dress, logos, or other discriminating marks, and indicia associated with Jill Conner Browne, the Sweet Potato Queens®, SPQ, Inc., and the Sweet Potato Queens' Website, LLC, are owned by Jill Conner Browne and/or SPQ, Inc. and may not be used without expressed prior written permission from Jill Conner Browne and/or SPQ, Inc.

For information about special discounts for bulk purchases,
please contact Simon & Schuster Special Sales at
1-800-456-6798 or business@simonandschuster.com.

Designed by Dana Sloan

Manufactured in the United States of America

10   9   8   7   6   5   4   3   2   1

Library of Congress Cataloging-in-Publication Data
Browne, Jill Conner.
   American thighs : the Sweet Potato Queens' guide to preserving your assets /
Jill Conner Browne.
       p.   cm.
   1. Aging—Humor.   2. Women—Humor.   I. Title.   II. Title: Sweet Potato
Queens' guide to preserving your assets.
   PN6231.A43B76   2009
   818'.5402—dc22   2008030675

ISBN-13: 978-0-7432-7838-6
ISBN-10:   0-7432-7838-0

Acknowledgments

When my very first book, *The Sweet Potato Queens' Book of Love*, was published, everybody, from family and friends to folks in the media, wanted to know "what's next." And I laughingly told them all that what I envisioned was a sort of "Nancy Drew" series, a seemingly endless stream of sagas about the Sweet Potato Queens—never dreaming it would actually come to pass. And yet here we are with book #8. Wow. It took a lot more than a village, lemme tell you—so here's this biggest THANK-YOU in the world to:

My ever cute and talented agent, Jenny Bent of Trident Media Group, who continues to be my invaluable friend, ally, and thinker-upper-of-stuff-for-me-to-do.

David Rosenthal, Denise Roy, Julia Prosser, Nicole De Jackmo, Kate Anofski, Deb Darrock, Aileen Boyle, Victoria Meyer, Leah Wasielewski, Sybil Pincus, Jackie Seow, and Dana Sloan—the esteemed and attractive team at Simon & Schuster who labor tirelessly on my behalf. I would also like to say a special thank-you to Honi Werner for her brilliant covers on *The First Big-Ass Novel* and *The Guide to Raising Children for Fun and Profit*, and to Janet Perr for stepping up to the plate and knocking it over the fence with the cover of this book.

Kyle Jennings and the staff at Bad Dog Management for innumerable services rendered, both mentionable and otherwise.

Alycia Jones and Sarajean Babin, who, along with their Spud Studs Russell and Mike, respectively, keep everything at www.sweetpotatoqueens.com going . . . somehow.

Theo Costas, John Rein, and the whole staff at Southern Beverage in Jackson, Mississippi, for their tremendous support of the SPQ® Million Queen March™. Show your own appreciation—buy somebody a Bud today, and get yourself a couple as well!

Jennifer Wall—the best little winemaker in the world—for bringing her fabulous Barefoot Wines and Bubbly—not to mention her very own Queenly self—to the SPQ® Million Queen March™.

Patty and Jeff Christie of Patty Peck Honda in Jackson, Mississippi, for their generous support of the SPQ® Million

Queen March™: has there EVER been a better time to drive a Honda? Get yours from these Queen-friendly folks!

Our very dear friend Henry Cooper, at Country Pleasin' Meats, who gave us the first annual Big-Ass Barbecue after the Parade this year. YUM and thank you!

Kenny Windham, Jan Michaels, and the whole crazy bunch at Clear Channel Radio in Jackson, Mississippi, for their overwhelming support all year long.

Liza and Rick Looser and their band of geniuses at the Cirlot Agency for TEN YEARS of brilliance that can be observed at www.sweetpotatoqueens.com!

The entire staff at the Hilton Jackson for cheerfully catering to the every whim of about ten thousand or so crazy women from all over the world on the third weekend of every March. Y'all are crazy—but in such a good way.

To the Royalest and Loyalest Court any Queen ever had— Cynthia Speetjens, Melanie Jeffreys, Pippa Jackson, Katie Werdel, George Ewing, Ellyn Weeks, Martha Jean Alford, and Robin Mitchell—who make it more fun every year, which ought to be impossible but apparently isn't.

To all of YOU—Queens everywhere, all over the world— who not only find, buy, read, and love my books but also share your unbelievably hilarious stories and heart-stoppingly fattening recipes with me—mmmmwaaaahh!

For Smokey Davis—who always insisted on being mentioned in my books. You left us way too soon, darlin'— and you took way too many good recipes with you.

Contents

Contents

Introduction

Although this book falls into the "NONFICTION" category, on account of I didn't make any of it up, I hope you are not looking to, like, LEARN a bunch of FACTS from it. If that was your expectation, then I hope that you have at least already paid for this book and that it is nonreturnable on account of my Plastic Surgery Fund needs all the help it can get. I am not a doctor nor do I play one on TV. There will be no medical advice herein—with the exception of repeated exhortations for you to "GO TO THE DOCTOR, YOU IDIOT." I hope you find that helpful.

This is sort of a Handbook and a Memoir for the Hot and Flashy—from the time we first felt the urge to put mascara on an eyelash and then bat it at somebody to the most recent time we looked in the mirror and tugged back on our neck and face skin to see what it would look like if we had a little "work" done. From the too-brief time in our youth that we actually looked "hot" and could pull off "flashy" without seeming pathetic—to the seemingly endless time in our later years when we only FEEL hot and that comes in flashes with buckets of sweat.

I will not be offering much in the way of "remedies" for any-thing that ails you—other than, hopefully, laughter, which I do believe is good for that, whatever it is.

I'm writing, of course, from the only perspective available to me—that of a woman completely stunned, stupefied, and not a little discombobulated and discomfited by the fact that she has personally passed into the latter range of that spectrum, and I'm writing with several goals in mind: to provide some much-needed laughs for my companions on the Twilight Path and some even-more-needed WARNINGS for our daughters, who are careening, willy-nilly and faster-than-they-will-ever-believe, in our direction. I hope to help some folks misspend their middle ages as blissfully as we misspent our youth and I hope to help keep some of the youngsters from spending their middle ages in bad relationships, jobs they hate, and/or prison (which is actually almost redundant).

To say that Youth is wasted on the Young has got to be THE understatement of all time. But a few too many of us are also not exactly taking advantage of all the wisdom we have suppos-edly been racking up in our inexorable trudge into Geezerdom. Appearances might suggest that some of us may not have learned ANYTHING of pith or import since we survived pu-berty.

If one is at all influenced by the cover stories on magazines available in the checkout lane at the grocery store, one could be convinced of one thing: Life Pretty Much Peaks in the Seventh Grade.

While waiting to pay for my weekly mountain of groceries, I gave a cursory glance to three different magazines—one for hip teens, one for hot twenties to forties, and one for perky geezers—and I was agog.

The teens were offered detailed instructions on achieving a HAIRSTYLE that would "get them what they wanted"—an arrangement of the hairs on their heads that would bring them all manner of success.

Hairstyle A would get them a job—not just "a" job, but THE job, the best one EV-ER. My husband, The Cutest Boy in the World, used to be a Human Resource Manager—he has never mentioned having studied cosmetology as a part of his education for this job. How did he know which candidate to hire without this info on Hot Hairstyles? And it couldn't be just a one-shot class either—hairstyles change—it would have to be a continuing education series for everyone in HR, would it not? Otherwise, the people with the best hair might not actually be selected for all the plum positions in Corporate America. And THEN what would happen? This could explain a lot about our current economy if you think about it.

Select B and you would instantly become irresistible to that certain guy. Okay, this could work. If all the guys who will date someone simply because of their great hairdos could be matched up with all the girls who will date somebody because they drive a hot car—well, it would take a whole big wad of Truly Shallow people out of the Dating Pool and that would have to be a boon to humankind.

Hairdo C promised you fame. I can't right off think of anybody who got famous only because of their hair—except for Rapunzel, there was her, but hey, happened once, could happen again, I guess. (Godiva does NOT count—nobody woulda cared about her hair if she hadn't been naked underneath it.)

But D, now, D was probably the one most often selected by teen girls across the USA. And I have to admit, it's the one that tempted me.

If you styled your hair like D, you would become known far and wide as The "IT" Girl. Oh. My. God. The IT Girl. I could be The IT Girl? And all it will take is this hairdo? I am so ready to be this, I am tempted to buy the magazine on the spot. Won't my friends and family be amazed when suddenly everybody in the world wants to look just like me—because I am THE IT GIRL? I grabbed the magazine off the rack and flipped it open to see for myself these amazingly powerful hairstyles, and of course there was a catch. FIRST you have to have about 850 times more hair on your head than I have on my whole body combined and it has to be thick and lustrous and very shiny. It also has to be about three feet long and platinum-blond. I am so not going to be The IT Girl by morning—or by the end of time as we know it. I imagine I am not the only one with dashed hopes in this regard.

My brief exam of the World Domination through Hairdos article did not give any info on which particular segments of the population (in this country or abroad) are especially susceptible to being held in total thrall by the Powerfully Coiffed, so if you do happen to be one of those individuals bountifully blessed by the Hair Gods/Goddesses and therefore capable of achieving and maintaining a Dominating Do, there was no hint as to where you might need go to sign up for The Job, to meet That Guy, or to catch the eye of any of the media, let alone commence being The IT Girl.

I'm sorry to be the one to tell you this—if you bought that magazine and have been disappointed by the overwhelming lack of worldwide response to your new hairdo—but I think you've been had.

Also in the publication for Hot Teens, there was one section devoted to teen boys who were invited to write in with questions about their own bodies. Who is surprised that there was a "size" question? Who is surprised that, once again, the response was "it doesn't matter"? Who agrees with that? Same answer for all of the above: nobody.

The magazine for hot twenties to forties promised to tell me what my hairstyle reveals about me as a person. (Besides the easily observable facts that I am inept, lazy, and have only about four hairs, and not particularly thick, lustrous, and/or shiny ones at that.) Of course, I had to flip that one open to see what my constant ponytail was telling the world about my innermost thoughts, and I was somewhat tickled to learn that ponytail wearers are considered to be quite hot in the sack. Yay, me!

But then I read on regarding the other dos and discovered that all the other hairstyles also revealed the sexy nature of the woman. What it eventually boiled down to, as far as I could tell, is that all women with hair on their heads of any kind are just rarin' to go, night and day. (Clearly, some guy wrote this, hoping to work a little subliminal suggestion on us.)

That was certainly a letdown, to discover that there was nothing special about me and my ratty-ass ponytail after all. I sought solace and inspiration from the "Spiritual" section in the same magazine. The way the table of contents described it, it sounded as if they had a full-time goddess on the payroll, dispensing life-changing nuggets of wisdom as needed. Okay— hook me up. I eagerly flipped over to her page and I am totally 100 percent NOT kidding you—this is what it said: "SASSY SAYING: MEOW."

Right off the bat, I gotta tell you, I HATE the word *sassy*. People are always trying to get me to buy clothes that are "sassy" or get a "sassy" haircut or come meet up with some other people, all of whom are just as "sassy" as they can be. I am NOT sassy, have not ever been sassy, nor do I aspire to be nor could I ever fool anybody anywhere into perceiving me to be sassy if I wanted to which I don't. I actively RESIST sass in all its forms and mutations. "Sassy" evokes a response in me much like "good luck" brought out in Holden Caulfield. I just wanna smack you upside your sassy head with a big ole sassy sack full of sassy rocks.

"Sassy" sounds cute and perky and swishy—bouncy hair, giggly voice, big crinkly petticoats, patent leather shoes. If you tried to make me sassy, I would look like the world's biggest fifth grader. A big oaf in a sassy suit. I don't wanna hang out with sassy people because the disparity between their sassiness and my non- is too great and glaring. I appear even larger than I actually am—which is huge. Plus I often find their perkiness to be a tad too much on the little-yap-dog side for me personally. I like my people—and my dogs—a little more laid-back.

So anyway, I was taken aback by the whole idea that their big goddess guru was offering me an axiom with a lead-in containing the word *sassy*—I cannot recall ever coming across references to SASSY, pro or con, in any spiritual-type book of ANY persuasion. I have actually met THE Dalai Lama in person and heard him speak, and as hilarious as he was, he never used *sassy* even ONE TIME in his whole talk. (Perhaps he'll work it into future talks since it seems to be quite the buzzword these days.)

But I was completely floored to further discover that the "mantra" their Spiritual Writer was serving up was your basic, unadulterated "MEOW." Meow? What does that even purport to MEAN in that context? Once again I am faced with the Question that has dogged me my entire life on this planet— WHAT WERE THEY THINKING? I can tell you what I am thinking—I am thinking that ALL of these magazine articles are written by the seventh-grade class at a New York junior high school.

At this point, I am GLAD I'm no longer young. I am relieved at having finally come to accept the truth about my hair— it will never BE full and foxy, no matter what the Fall Forecast for Hair Fashion may dictate. I am thankful that my next book contract will not be influenced in any way by my hairstyle or lack thereof. (Unless the publisher is a ponytail freak, in which case, I am SO IN.) I don't think I ever in my life "got a man" because of my hair—I hope not anyway. That's just not much to live up to, is it?

I am feeling much smarter, more highly evolved, on a lofty spiritual plane—quite smug in my antisassiness and near-baldness. At least I know that even a well-placed "meow" availeth little, unless you're in dire need of a saucer of milk.

So what did the near-geezer mag have to offer me, a qualified reader? Two titillating headlines on the cover grabbed my eye immediately. First, there was an article on "waist management"—har-de-har-har—"waist"—get it? and THEN— even better—FIND A THERAPIST NEAR YOU.

Okay, so the magazine rack takes us straight from the seventh grade to welcoming Death with no indication that there was anything much in between. Surely there must be?

Is it possible that, as a species, we're not actually capable of emotional growth past puberty? That if we live to be a hundred, we'll be just as goofy as we were at thirteen? On the one hand, that's depressing—on the other, it could be the best news ever. We could all just relax and accept our own personal igmonosity, and that of others would be far less irritating—if we just called bullshit on the whole idea of ever Growing Up and just eliminated all expectation of Maturity.

This may be an idea whose time has come—and what, you may well ask, does any of this have to do with THIGHS, American or otherwise, and the means by which we might strive to preserve these and any and all Other Assets? Excellent question.

Well, you prolly never really thought about it before but—when you do think about it—THIGHS (more specifically, women's thighs) are really a major factor in just about every aspect of our daily lives. I would rank them second only to our hormones in level of importance and influence on the Universe as we know it.

I can hear you asking, "Is she SERIOUS?" Naaahhh, not really. However, I have found that thighs, most often my own, but not infrequently those of others as well, have, in fact, played and continue to play a fairly significant role in all phases of my life. (Thighs as birth control, for example. Pretty efficient when used [as in "closed"] regularly—but backup is highly recommended.) This is not a whole book about thighs, obviously, but I think the subject bears some examination—in terms of discussion only, of course; no way am I bringing out my actual THIGHS for examination—not even if you're blind.

1

Hair of the Dog Is Actually a Drink, Not a Coiffure

Of course, my OWN personal hairs, all four of them, would be rejected by any self-respecting dog and I've actually seen any number of dogs with whom I would happily trade hair, if they were to offer, but it has long been a source of confusion and amazement to me, the stuff that people with what I consider to be enviable hairs will do to 'em in what appears to be a deliberate attempt to fuck 'em up. Or perhaps they've had the feeling that they were just looking too damn smart and are just looking to "dumb down" their appearance as much as possible.

In 1979, Bo Derek did the impossible: she ran down a beach—in slow motion—in a very revealing swimsuit—in broad daylight, no less—in front of a MOVIE camera—and she looked mind-numbingly gorgeous doing it. There's a logical explanation for her ability to do these things, of course: she sold her soul to the Devil. No mortal woman living in 1979 could have done such a thing. Sure, today you've got your Camerons and your Venuses—superstars of screen and sports—who have actual human bodies that could bear up to such baring, but exercise and healthful eating had not yet been invented in 1979. Bulimia hadn't even been born yet. So there you have it, devil-spawn not human girl—no comparison. Aren't you glad now you didn't slash your wrists after you watched *10*?

The other thing that the Bo-demon did that has wreaked havoc on humanity for lo, these many years, was she actually looked GOOD in that ridiculous hairdo. By the time you read this, it will have been a good thirty YEARS since that movie was released, and STILL TODAY, at least 78 percent of all tourists to tropical locales will come home with their hair in a Bo-Do and absolutely 100 percent, if not more, of them will look like complete morons.

This continues to mystify me. I mean, I can't recall ever seeing a BLIND tourist with a Bo-Do, and that would be the only understandable explanation for it, to my way of thinking—if an unscrupulous beachside cosmetologist were to perpetrate this heinous hairdo on a vulnerable and unsuspecting visually impaired person. Because why would anybody with one or two WORKING eyeballs EVER submit themselves to it after having SEEN it done on someone else—on account of, in the EN-tire history of HAIR—not nobody, not no-how, ain't NEVER looked

GOOD in the Bo-Do, 'ceptin' for the Bo herownself and she was a succubus so no fair.

I have never before or since seen in person another actual human person who I believe WOULD look good in the Bo-Do so I don't think you should go off down there and be led, by Demon Rum or anybody else, to believe that YOU are the exception to this rule. If your friends think it would be funny to ply you with tequila and leave you passed out in the clutches of the Bo-Do person—well, I agree, it prolly will be pretty funny. But if they don't also FORCE you to UN-do it before you board the homebound plane, they are really not your friends at all and your life will be immeasurably improved if you put them under a restraining order to keep them at an acceptable distance.

Even MEN fall prey to the Bo-Do, which has been perhaps an even greater unexplained mystery of the universe. Why would any GUY want to look like Bo Derek? Well, upon further consideration, I do know a few—quite a few—GAY men who would kill Barbra Streisand if doing so would enable them to look like Bo Derek, but they have, it must be said, even LESS of a chance at achieving this than any of US. And yet the island resorts are overpopulated with white males sporting Bo-Dos.

It does appear, thankfully, that the Moe-Do is dying away. For a while there every third guy you saw had his hair inexplicably styled like Moe—as in Three Stooges Moe. Now, there's a look for you. Or maybe I'm missing something—was the legendary Moe reputed to be a major cocksman of his time? That might—

no, that WOULD—explain it—men will do ANY-thing if they think it holds even a very remote possibility of leading them to the top of some woman's thighs. So far, as far as I know, there ain't no mountain high, ain't no valley low, ain't no river wide, no, and there ain't no haircut hilarious—enough to discourage them in this, their lifelong relentless quest. Thank GOD.

So which one of you bitches tricked 'em into the new Gerber Baby–Do? Come on—fess up—I KNOW YOU DID IT! You cannot turn on a TV or open a magazine without having to look at some dumb-ass grown-up MAN—with all his hair combed into a VERTICAL POINT in the MIDDLE of his head. I am not kidding—go right now and look. Now TELL me you could take that guy seriously enough to wind up in bed with him. You can-NOT make me believe it. Next you'll be telling me you'd do a three-way with Ed Grimley and Alfalfa! (If you're too young to know who Ed Grimley is, Google him and get back to me. And if you're THAT young, you REEEALLY don't know who Alfalfa is, so Google him as well, but you gotta put in "The Little Rascals," too, or you're gonna get some kind of sprout instead of the world's earliest-known nerd.)

So, whoever you are out there who's convinced all these guys to commit this hair-trocity—why not push it a little further and get 'em to go all-out-Ed-Grimley and start wearing their pants up under their armpits and all? Come to think of it—that WOULD eliminate the proliferation of butt cracks we've been forced to view the last few years, revealed by the enduring but baffling "fad" of wearing your pants in such a way as to offer ease to anyone interested in making you their jail-house bitch.

How THAT caught on is one of your REAL, big-time mysteries. And that is where it started—in prison—where belts are taboo—the male inmates wishing to establish an intimate connection with others would telegraph this fact by wearing their pants twenty-five sizes too big so that they were always pre-yanked down—got the word out and saved time and effort, too. Win-win.

Only somehow it mutated out into the free world, the result being that one cannot even indulge that time-honored tradition of dead-cat slinging without being presented with some guy's nekkid butt crack, and when is the last time it was one you were glad you got to see?

Color at ANY Cost

I personally know of two (2) different women who have actually RISKED their very LIVES just to get a little bit blonder. My very own daughter, Bailey, was in the middle of having her blond-ness emphasized recently when a customer came careening into the shop, crying, "TAKE COVER! TAKE COVER! THERE'S

A TORNADO!" And indeed, there was. Bailey said it was absolutely terrifying—they heard the telltale freight-train roar that survivors invariably describe after these horrific storms—they saw the roof blow off the building next to them, heard the explosion of all the cars' windows in the parking lot—as they frantically raced to the back of the building to seek shelter. "Thank God you're safe," was naturally my response, to which SHE replied, "OMIGOD, Mom, yes, and Christa is so great, she was able to get us back there right by the sinks so when my timer went off, she could rinse me—I just knew I was going to get blown away with that bleach on my hair!"

I apologized for my shocking lapse—chagrined that I, her very own mother, could be so thoughtless that, upon learning she had suffered so close a brush with a killer storm, I did not first inquire as to what effect, if any, this whole experience might have had on the condition of her HAIR. My goodness, what a close call indeed. I didn't say this to her, of course, not wishing to upset my high-strung child any further, but I trembled as I thought to myself, "Why, WHAT if she'd been late for her appointment and the whole salon had just been wiped off the parking lot? Christa—easily the best colorist in town—would have been blown to bits and, lord knows, it would have been waaaay too late for her to get in with any other reputable salon—she could have had darkish roots for WEEKS!" Man, you just never know what's around that corner waiting for you, do you? Some serious life lessons for us all here—well, all of us who have color-assisted hair, anyway.

Our next Blond-ee was well into her process, foils on her head, timer set, when her Blond-er got a phone call. The ever-vigilant Blond-er shrewdly took the timer with her when she was summoned to the front of the shop to answer the call, so she didn't run the risk of becoming distracted and leaving the blonding on too long, which can result in a nice SINK full of perfectly blonded hair—and a VERY crabby Blond-ee.

Long before the buzzer even went off, the Blond-er returned to her station, only to discover that her Blond-ee was, there is no way to sugarcoat this, throwing up BLOOD into the shampoo basin. Astutely observing that this was not your run-of-the-mill bad-hangover situation here but your genuine life-threatener, Blond-er rightly took it upon herownself to summon an ambulance for her Blond-ee in distress. Wouldn't you KNOW it, the EMTs got there JUST as the timer went off.

Blond-ee flatly refused to get on the gurney until the Blond-er rinsed her out. She didn't feel like it WAS her day to die, but by God, if it WAS, she wasn't going out with black roots OR bald.

Well, they didn't know they were headed out to put their lives on the line when they left the house for the beauty parlor that morning—but that's the way it turned out, and you may be surprised to learn, as we do from these examples, that our strongest human drive is NOT, as previously thought, Survival but rather Blond Roots.

I apologize for the fact that I have not heard any similar tales of dedicated Brunettes—no, wait a minute, I do know one—and it's a good'un, too! Okay, to be completely honest here, the perpetrator of this hirsute crime of passion was a natural-born brunette, although it did require some high-dollar salon work to perpetuate that condition at the time of this story.

Whoo-Hoo Hoo-Hoo!

Our dear friend and mentor, Miss Lydy—the very one who taught us in *The Sweet Potato Queens' Book of Love* about the Five Men We Must Have in Our Lives at All Times—although, if you'll recall, I did not give her actual credit for it in that book, thinking, WRONGLY—SOOO VERY, VERY WRONGLY— that Miss Lydy might be shy about having her name out there, attached to that story. Upon publication of that first book, I was informed, hotly so, by Miss Lydy that I'd best be givin' credit where credit was due, first chance I got, and boy-hidee, did I ever! Next book out—*God Save the Sweet Potato Queens*—I made sure I not only acknowledged, I verbally bowed and scraped before the feet of, the exalted Most High Miss Lydy. And, true to form, she not only forgave my lapse but gave me more fodder.

Now, Miss Lydy was, truth be told, a tad bit older than most of us who hung around worshipping her. I'm not real sure if anybody was actually well informed as to her age, but she did allow as to how she did have her some REEEALLY old friends. She was laughing fit to kill one day as she hung up the phone from talking to one of 'em. Seems the Old Friend Girlene had her a new Old Beau who had been sparkin' her along quite regular and Girlene was thinking that Tonight might just be The Night and she was all excited but then she remembered something that sorta debloomed her rose, at least temporarily—but, as is so typical of her resourceful generation, no sooner had the problem presented itself than she had thought up—and executed—the very cleverest of solutions.

Miss Lydy was almost laughing too hard to explain—almost. Okay, Girlene was all hot and six kinds of ready for a very-long-awaited trot until she remembered that it had, in fact, been a really long wait in between suitors—so long she couldn't really precisely say that she could right off remember when she had Received Her Last Gentleman Caller but she was pretty sure that whenever it was, she had still possessed a full crop of down-there hair that matched her hair-hair, black for black.

Now, here she was, however many years later, and her hair-hair was still as black as black could ever hope to be—but her hoo-hoo hair was, well, GONE. It had done got tired a-waitin' and flown the hoo-hoo coop. And now she had a bona fide Gentleman Caller and here she sat with her head full of bootblack hair and her hoo-hoo bald as an egg. What to do? What to do?

They don't call 'em the Greatest Generation for NOTHIN', you know! She did what anybody with an ounce of spunk and a brand-new Sharpie would do! She drew some on!

A lesser woman woulda blown Jack Daniel's out her nose upon hearing that story, but Miss Lydy would NEVER waste good whiskey. Nor would she keep a PRICELESS story to herself. I expressed my own personal hope that somebody told Girlene the truth that would relieve her mind and save her Sharpies—that what she was sitting on was a PAIN-FREE, ALL-NATURAL Brazilian! I was assured, with a derisive snort, that "they read *Cosmo*, TOO, y'know!" Girlene just thought the old boy might need some kind of landmark until he sorta got the lay of the land, so to speak.

Sadly, tragically, Miss Lydy is no longer with us. At least not where we can see her and hug her. But obviously, the woman was a force of nature—so I've NO DOUBT she's with us—there's no place big enough to HOLD her. Whenever I go to a play anywhere—but especially when I go to her beloved New Stage Theater in Jackson, Mississippi, where she starred in and stole many a show—I swear I can just hear her saying what she believed with all her might: "LOOK AT THIS! ISN'T THIS GREAT? PANTIES IN THE BUSHES—EVERYBODY'S SCREWING EVERYBODY! IT'S . . . THE THEATER!" Amen.

The Color Purple, Revisited

And then there's Mary Katherine. She and Bailey have been friends for a goodly part of their young lives and you know how your kids have one or two friends that you just LOVE yourown-self? Kids you would hang out with on your own—whether your kid was around or not? Mary Katherine is one of those kids—she's destined to be one of those people—the ones whom EV-ERYBODY JUST LOVES. Mary Katherine is like my friend Katie who I've told you about—who is the World's Most Perfect Person—literally every single person who has EVER MET Katie loves her to death. No, really, like we would DIE for her, she's so perfect. Really. Mary Katherine is gonna be that same way. You just have to smile when you see her. Especially if you see her, like, now.

You would smile if you saw her now because she is completely purple—head to toe—hair, skin, nails—all but her teeth and the whites of her eyes—she is purple. Not blotchy or patchy—she's a smooth, consistent, really quite lovely shade of purple. Like Blue Man Group—only just the one girl and purple. Like a Smurfette—only purple. The part in her hair is a bit vivid—kinda looks like maybe Girlene got after her with a neon purple Sharpie—but other than that, she is a perfect monochrome of purple.

It seems that Bailey went by to pick up Mary Katherine—who was still white at curbside but had some kind of goo on her hair, which she said she would deal with when they got to our house. Bailey said fine but they had to pick up Jodie on the way. Mary Katherine was getting just a wee bit antsy about whatever it was that was on her hair. So much so that upon entering our house, she bee-lined it straight into MY bathroom and hopped in the shower. Fortunately for all concerned, neither The Cutest Boy in the World nor I were in the shower at the time.

Jodie went upstairs to shower in Bailey's bathroom and Bailey just flopped on MY bed—again, it was fortuitous that TCBITW and I were elsewhere that evening—turned on *Law & Order* and forgot about Mary Katherine for a time. Eventually, the sound of the continuously running shower registered in her brain and she realized that Mary Katherine had been in there for what seemed an inordinately long time. And about that time, the water stopped, the shower door opened, and the screaming began.

"BAILEY! BAILEY! BAILEY! OMIGOD! BAILEY!" And just as Jack McCoy was saying something really important to Lennie Briscoe, too. Bailey grudgingly hit the pause button and opened the door to the bathroom—and there before her stood a screaming, naked, purple girl. It was Mary Katherine—only purple and hysterical.

Mary Katherine learned—as did we all that night—that there is a most EXCELLENT reason why they have black shampoo sinks at beauty salons—and there is also a most EXCEL-

LENT reason why they have you lean waaaay back and put your head over in there, and that same most EXCELLENT reason applies to how come they have you put on a smock over your clothes, and it's why they wear gloves when they fool with your hair while it's got the goo on it. That most EXCELLENT reason is that it's DYE.

No one knows, no one will ever know—probably including Mary Katherine—exactly why it was that she wanted to dye her hair purple that night. But no one will ever forget it. Certainly not her—I don't think anything in life will ever surprise her quite as much as realizing she had dyed her EN-tire body purple. Not Bailey—one is never really adequately prepared to segue with no preamble from a Jack McCoy monologue to a dripping purple screamer in your mother's bathroom. Not the folks at the Cherokee who called her "Oompa-Loompa" all night. And not me either—I've got the purple shower to remind me.

Hair Today, Gone Momentarily

If Mother Nature had wanted you to have hair (anywhere), She would have given it to you (and left it there), and apparently She doesn't take kindly to poseurs of any kind—given the wrack and ruin we see visited on those of us who have tried to convince the world that we are anything that we are not—from big-busted to blond (or purple, as the case may be). She also apparently does not care for us to pretend that we have hair—hoo-hoo or head—as we shall see from the following testimony.

Queen Martha once got herself a very fine head of on-again, off-again big blond hair in the form of a very fine wig. She did love prancing around, feeling so foxy and fine with that big-ass blond wig.

Speaking of "big ass," let me pause for a moment here and explain something to folks in Other Parts of the Country who may have been baffled by the Southern Woman's undying devotion to Big Hair. Here's the deal: it's not so much that we necessarily love Big Hair for its own sake as we do what it does for our overall balance. Bottom line—Big Hair makes your butt look smaller.

I myownself am a proponent of not only Big Hair but also long jackets on account of my butt is so huge, if I were to put on hair big enough to balance the thing, I would not be able to fit in normal-sized automobiles, and forget about walking through standard-sized doorways. So, I will put on my travel hair, which, at the very least, quadruples the size of my own hair, and then completely cover my overly ample ass with a very long jacket. I feel so strongly about my personal need for long jackets that I will tell you flat-out, if I am ever found dead wearing a short jacket, you will know that I was dead before that jacket went on.

So anyway, Queen Martha had her a big-ass blond wig. (I'm certain her ass was just as tiny as a little ole baby butter bean and she really did not need any balancing for it a-tall.) She was in full party-prance across a crowded patio once, and she admits to being somewhat distracted—okay, she was completely mesmerized—by her own fetching reflection in the big sliding glass doors, when her prance carried her directly under a hanging basket full of ferns—which would have posed no clearance problem for her without her augmented hair situation, but as it was . . . Yes, she continued moving forward while her supplemental hair remained hanging right along with the basket, swaying slightly in the soft breeze.

Now, everybody's worn a hat or cap of some kind at some time or other, so you know either firsthand or by casual observation the devastating effects they have on hairdos. Hat hair is hideous—all flat and greasy-looking—which is probably why you had the hat on to begin with, to hide your already flat and greasy-looking hair—so when you take the hat off, that condition is significantly exacerbated.

If you've never personally had occasion to wear a wig, let's have a word about "wig head." Multiply the Hideous Factor of Hat Hair by the biggest number you can think of—then double it. When you take a wig off, it makes your hair look like Girlene's pubes—or perhaps Trent Lott's hair—like it was drawn on with a Sharpie.

This was the vision of herself that Queen Martha viewed in the patio doors—that and the doubled-over figures of her fellow partygoers. She can't clearly recall which sound was louder—her own shriek of horror or the hysterical hee-haws of the onlookers—they still echo like the howling of hellhounds in her memory.

Horribly Hairifying

But Queen Martha's wig woes were nothing compared to what happened to another Queen who will mercifully remain nameless. Well, we'll call her Tammy, just because it's a name we all know, love, and identify closely with.

Let me set the stage for you here. In the early sixties, when Big Hair was born, thanks to Jackie Kennedy and her enviable bouffant, many trade tricks were developed for hair enlargement. Singer Dusty Springfield had a truly amazing coiffure featuring big bouffs in several locations on her head—front, back, top, sides—an architectural wonder is all it was and the whole world of women was dead to copy it, and this included our Queen Tammy.

I have no idea how Dusty achieved her look—she had, after all, I'm sure, a team of hair professionals laboring night and day to maintain it—but the style inevitably trickled down to the aspiring fashion plates of a certain high school in Florence, Alabama—of which our Tammy was but one—however, a dedicated and very enthusiastically creative one.

Tammy found that by employing an ingenious combination

of tools readily available even in Florence, Alabama, she could erect an almost exact replica of the coveted Dusty Springfield Bouffant on her very own personal head. The first item she needed was a couple of wiglets. Wiglets were an early incarnation of Travel Hair—small handfuls of hair that one could secure at various points on one's head to supplement the supply of hair growing naturally. They came in about four colors and looked vaguely reminiscent of hair, and so if you stuck it underneath some of your actual hair and combed over it, satisfactory blending could be accomplished and a desirable pouf achieved.

But even with the addition of three or four wiglets' worth of hair, Tammy's hair could not be harassed into the desired height for the Dusty Springfield. Through what I'm sure was much trial and error—although after hearing this story, I'm wildly curious as to what all she REJECTED as an acceptable add-on— somehow Tammy made the unbelievable discovery that if she took an ordinary Kotex feminine napkin (I always loved that name) and pinned it TO THE TOP OF HER HEAD, she could then cover it with a combination of her own hair and her wiglets and VOYOLA—she could pass for Dusty Springfield anywhere, at least as far as hairstyles went.

A word about the Kotex thing. They were huge—like loaves of bread almost—minipads were decades away. I cannot personally imagine having enough hair growing on my head not only to attach three or four wiglets to—but then to also completely COVER a big giant Kotex with it? I'm thinking the head of hair that could do all THAT was plenty big to start with, and by the time she got done, her head musta looked like a hot-air balloon.

But anyway, she got away with this bizarre subterfuge for many, many months, to the mystified envy of all her friends. To NO ONE would she reveal the foundation of her very bouffiest of bouffants—and I can certainly understand her need for secrecy. And everything was fine, as they say, UNTIL . . . Her secret would probably have been safe for all eternity if she had just stayed off that roller coaster.

Uphill was fine but she lost one wiglet on the first downhill and one on nearly every subsequent scream-filled swoosh and turn. Of course, she and everybody else on the ride remained oblivious to the happenings on her head until they coasted back in to the starting point—where she arrived, bouffless, wearing nothing on her head but a big fluffy white Kotex pinned VERY SECURELY to the top of her head.

She got a pixie cut the very next day.

Asset-Preserving Tip

I just don't know what to tell you here. There doesn't seem to be anything anybody can do to dissuade us from committing the occasional follicular felony. I suppose if that's the dumbest thing we do, we could consider it a mercy. That's all I got. If I were to come up with some means of convincing us to give up the lifelong pursuit of unattainable hair perfection—however that manifests for each of us as unique and disturbed individuals—it would bankrupt a multibillion-dollar industry that's banking on that very pursuit, and I don't want THAT on my conscience.

Hit & Run
on Memory Lane

Vivid Memory: I am fourteen and therefore infinitely wise—and supremely confident in that wisdom. This wisdom renders me totally without patience where any Mere Ordinary Mortals might be concerned. (The Mere Ordinary Mortals group—MOM—being comprised primarily of My Mother, whose every communication with me is met with heaving sighs and rolling eyeballs.) I cannot—and really have no desire to—comprehend that any MOM may have, in fact, had an Actual Life before I and my contemporaries arrived on the scene. I cannot call up any vision of them, say, dancing with abandon, trying out the latest fashion, laughing over cocktails with girl-friends—and just forget about ANYTHING with BOYfriends.

No, in my fourteen-year-old mind's eye, the MOM have always done what my own personal MOM unit is doing right now—standing at the kitchen sink, washing the dishes from the supper they just cooked for and served to me. The MOM have always been here, serving me—in an endless cycle of cooking, cleaning, toting, and fetching—all centered, in my mind deservedly, around me. They did not exist before Me—because there was no Reason for them to do so. I Am—and therefore, So Are They. It is, and ever will be, ALL about ME.

Suddenly, the MOM at the kitchen sink speaks, no doubt in response to some insufferable teenage remark I have made in her direction. What she says will echo in my mind for decades to come. And with the passing of each consecutive decade, I will be reminded of what a complete and total asshole I was as a teenager and I will also become less and less confident that I have improved much in that time.

What the MOM says is this: "I don't really FEEL any different inside today—than I did when I was YOUR age." If she had picked up a pair of giant cymbals and crashed them together with my pinhead in between them, I don't think I could have been any more stupefied than I was by those words.

I turned slowly in my chair and looked at her back, saw that she was stooping slightly as she washed the dishes because at five feet eleven inches, the countertop was too low for her. I saw her gray hair—that had never in my memory been any other color. I saw her old lady clothes, covering her old lady body, her old lady feet splayed out in her old lady shoes. She was, after all,

OVER forty, and therefore, in my mind, as good as dead—and yet she had just said out loud to me that SHE still felt exactly the same TODAY as she did when she was MY AGE.

My first thought, of course, was that she meant she had always FELT the way she LOOKED to me. I visualized her going to her high school pep rallies in her "old lady comfort" (that is what she called 'em) shoes and her old lady dresses with her old lady gray hair maybe pulled back in a pathetic attempt at a perky ponytail. I could just see her standing there, perhaps with some clothes for the dry cleaners under one arm, a pile of discarded newspapers under the other, looking preoccupied—not cheering for the team but rather, perhaps, wondering if she'd remembered to take anything out of the freezer to cook for supper—and impatiently waiting for all these people to clear out so she could get her vacuuming done, and didn't anybody EVER think to wipe their feet—what, were they born in a barn? And did they have to be so LOUD? Don't be making all that racket in here— go out in the yard if you want to act like wild animals—and DON'T SLAM THE DOOR! And don't be jumping around like that, you're gonna put somebody's eye out—don't come crying to ME when you break your neck! Go back and change clothes, miss priss, you're gonna freeze your japonica* in that skirt.

---

* Frozen japonica—Childhood memory: unexpected cold snap caused damage to a neighbor's shrub—I heard her complaining to Mama that "it was so cold last night, my japonica froze." I did not realize she was referring to her camellia bush.

Don't leave all this mess for ME to clean up—I KNOW y'all don't leave this kinda mess at DARLENE'S house—I am NOT your MAID!

Of course, in my imagination, all her contemporaries (the Mere Ordinary Mortals/mothers of my friends)—THEY all appeared to be young and vital, like so many puppies cavorting happily in the sunshine. My own mother is the only one in my mind who was born Old. From the vantage point afforded me by my staggering teenage conceit, I simply could not conceive of HER EVER having been young.

And yet here she is—telling me not only WAS she young— but she STILL FEELS THAT WAY. I could scarcely breathe—it gave me an attack of claustrophobia. Now I saw her as a young person trapped in the body of an old woman and she seemed to me to be like someone sentenced to life in prison without parole—life was going on as usual all around her, but she could not get out of that wrecked cage of a body to which she'd been consigned forever.

Like *The Man in the Iron Mask*—only she was The Woman in the Flabby Body—just as horrifying a fate, in my opinion. Actually worse. At least nobody but the prison staff ever SAW the Man in the Iron Mask—my Mother, on the other hand, had to go out every day in public and be SEEN—IN THAT TERRIBLE BODY—IN THOSE AWFUL OLD LADY CLOTHES— and here she is telling me that she still FEELS like she's a teenager. Oh, the horror!

I imagine if I myself had to even walk out in the front YARD in that housedress, with those shoes and that hair—in that BODY—well, I would just rather be dead and by the quickest, most private means possible—and then, if you would, please, just cremate the wretched remains on the spot.

Self-satisfied in my all-consuming Teenage Smug, I somehow subconsciously believed that I personally would not EVER age, that MY skin would remain sleek and taut around my ever-lean frame, that MY muscles would always promptly obey whatever command my ever-sharp brain issued and that MY perky tits and ass would ever BE perky. I didn't imagine that the MOM felt any sense of grief or loss at her own condition because, in my mind, it had not changed. It wasn't like she ever once HAD anything like my own exquisite perfection and had somehow allowed it to deteriorate—to me, she'd always BEEN just as she was NOW. "When you got nothin', you got nothin' to lose"—seemed apropos.

On the other hand, I had another parent—my in-house representative of the Doting and Delightfuls (DAD), who always seemed handsome and dashing to me—and so that got me to thinking—how did this old lady snag such a PRIZE? He didn't strike me as having a Granny Complex, and yet here he was, blissfully wedded to the hag I saw at the sink. Hmmmm.

And so to the old family albums I went, and for the first time, I actually SAW the people in the photos that did not contain ME. At any past perusals, any photos lacking my gracious presence were thumbed past quickly—blah, blah, blah, crowd noise, crowd noise, crowd noise—ahhh—here we are now— ME, ME, ME!

Suddenly, the young GIRL playing with her dog, trying on a funny hat, making faces for the camera, skiing, sailing, riding horses, smiling ear-to-ear—that young GIRL became real to me. And she was followed closely by the young WOMAN— dressed to kill, makeup and hair perfect, posing with one handsome young man after another, until finally there was just One Handsome Young Man over and over in the photos—and I easily recognized HIM as my very own darlin' Daddy. And there he was, in the Stork Club in New York City—grinning, with his arm around that beautiful young woman. And there he was, bundled up in his Navy peacoat and watch cap, playing in the blinding snow with that same radiant young woman. And there he was, beaming an impossibly broad grin, with his new bride— that same gorgeous young woman—the MOM.

Oh. My. God. I now KNEW how she got him . . . MOM was HOT.

Mom was hot. Mom was hot. MOM! WAS! HOT! Holy shit! Ho-ly SHIT! I'm talking MOM here—do you understand me? MOM! My MOM—THAT one over there—frump woman, the cook, the housekeeper, the rule-maker, killer-of-all-teenage-joy—MOM—was NOT ALWAYS a Mere Ordinary Mortal— she USED TO BE HOT!

And that's kinda sorta when I knew—if it happened to

her—it could happen to me. And isn't Karma just the biggest bitch in the Universe?

Of COURSE, it IS happening to ME—I can only pitifully pray at this point that I DON'T get all that I so richly DESERVE, Karmically speaking. I look in the mirror and I feel a Mr. Bill moment coming on—"Ooooooooohhhh, noooooooo!" And I realize as I write this—there are MILLIONS of people out there who are TOO FUCKING YOUNG to even KNOW WHO MR. BILL IS . . . was . . . OOOOOOOHHHH, NOOOOOOO!

It always felt like I was, oh, like, sort of IT, y'know? The Universe just more or less culminated with me and my generation and we couldn't really see any NEED—let alone likelihood— that there would actually BE more generations after us and we certainly never foresaw that WE would move inexorably into the slot FORMERLY occupied by our MOMS and DADS—that WE would become the inhabitants of Geezerville. And yet here we are—the train has screeched to a halt and we have all been herded off onto the platform in the freezing rain and the sign on the station clearly reads, WELCOME TO GEEZERVILLE—NOW LET'S SEE HOW YOU LIKE IT, YOU SNOTTY LITTLE SHITS! And we can hear our parents snickering from the shadows.

We are all wailing, "OOOOOOOOHHHH, NOOOO-OOO!" and laughing hysterically at this joke for the ten-thousandth time—and the young folks riding away on the train have no earthly idea what is so fucking funny about "Ooooohhh, noooooo!"—or how we could find ANYTHING to even SMILE about at this point in our lives, since we all look pretty well done-for in their opinion.

Okay, so I have come face-to-face with proof positive that my own personal mama was, in truth, once a young and vibrant being and there is also a fair pile of pretty convincing evidence that one of the two persons largely responsible for any loss of said youth and vibrancy would most definitely be memyownself. (By the way, for the record, somewhere along the way Mama stopped being a Mere Ordinary Mortal in my estimation and became an almost godlike creature of infinite wisdom and valuable experience. I'm pretty sure her elevation probably coincided not surprisingly with the birth of my OWN daughter and the stunning realization that I was myownself soon to become someone else's Mere Ordinary Mortal and the object of all HER scorn and derision. Experience is the best source of Empathy, is it not?)

So, from gazing in gape-mouthed disbelief at the photographic proof of Mama's former fabulosity, the natural progression took me to my OWN photo albums containing substantiation for the possibility that what went around had indeed come around and that Mama wasn't the ONLY old gray mare that ain't what she used to be, many long years ago.

There I was in photo after photo taken at beaches and pools, local and worldwide, wearing as little as possible—and looking pretty good in it (or out of it, as the case may have been), fairly flawless thighs included—but what was the source of that mysterious total body sheen, glimmering in the sun? My über-tan body did not appear to be so much WET as it did, well, GREASY.

Oh, yes. I remember now. Wherever we were, we baked in the sun for HOURS on end, day after day, all summer long, every summer. We didn't even actually wait for summer to officially arrive. If we got a chance to go to the beach and it was only 60 degrees but sunny—we would dig a body-sized hole in the sand and stretch out in it, out of the wind, and toastily roast ourselves in the pit.

We not only worshipped the sun—we offered our bodies up as greased sacrifices to it by covering our exposed skin—which was mostly all the skin we individually possessed—with BABY OIL. Ever put butter on a chicken before you bake it? Gives you that delicious golden-brown CRISPY skin—mmm-hmmm—that's what we did to our very own skin that we knew full well we were gonna have to live in for the REST of our lives. But did we pay any attention to what all that broiling was doing to us? Beyond the fact that it made us look golden brown and delicious? Nah. We paid no attention at all to the CRISPY part, and tha-a-a-at's the part that's taught us the true meaning of the words "rue the day." We are rueing all those days Big Time. Every time I look in the mirror, it is rue-time again for sure. And while it is still possible for me—should I discard caution completely—to achieve that golden-brown part, I'm pretty sure my delicious days are done. Sigh.

As I reminisce about both the baby oil and the thin thighs of my youth—I preach and carp and rant without ceasing on both subjects to my own daughter, Bailey, who at twenty still possesses those perfect thighs and that crease-free skin. In a version of "scared straight" tactics, I regularly show her my own thighs as a terrifyingly dire warning of what COULD lie ahead for her if she is less than vigilant in both her exercise regimen and eating habits as well as her SPF selection.

She and her friends will be putting on their teeny-tiny bikinis—oh! It is one of the heartbreaks of my old age that I can no longer in good conscience put on a teeny-tiny bikini and go outside in it—and I'll hear them clumping and giggling down the stairs in their sandals and sunglasses, all set to sun themselves by the lake. I jump out in front of them, lifting my calf-length old-lady-version-of-a-sundress high above my crinkly, wrinkly, baggy, saggy knees—and higher still, exposing a great expanse of enormous, quivering, gelatinous THIGHS, and I say, "THIS, little girls, is what YOU'RE gonna GET if you don't start paying attention NOW!" (in my best "I'll-get-you-my-pretty-and-your-little-dog-too voice)—and when they stop retching and resume normal breathing, I drop my skirt and repeat my eat-right-work-out-and-always-ALWAYS-ALWAYS-wear-sunscreen spiel. If I can save even one young woman from those THIGHS, I will not have lived in vain.

Asset-Preserving Tip

Karma does not like Smug. If you do, for some reason, happen to be one of the lucky ones who glides through five or six decades relatively unscathed, do NOT be risking a rotator cuff injury patting yourself on the back. Also, do not be preaching the gospel of eating right, getting regular exercise, and popping vitamins as the Way, the Truth, and the Life for all those who would desire to live forever still able to fit into their high school prom dress. Karma is listening and she has ears like a bat. You do NOT want to attract her attention.

3

No Matter What Skin You're In

Y ou've got to live in it your whole EN-tire life, so consider yourself behooved to taking great good care with it and of it. Our mamas didn't know any better than to let everybody, themselves and us, get chargrilled every summer of the world up until about 1997 or thereabouts, when a few people did start to acknowledge the existence of melanoma.

When I was growing up, the sole summer goal of every person living was to get their skin deeply bronzed and/or mahoganized as quickly as possible. For many hapless white people, this was and is simply a physical impossibility—not that they allowed the absolute absence of melanin in their skin to serve as any kind of deterrent or discouragement. To the contrary— they were the most determined of all. I grew up with people so white-skinned as to render them utterly UN-tannable, under any circumstances—if you were to just try to PAINT them brown, it would take repeated heavy coats of enamel to cover their whiteness. And yet every single solitary summer of their lives, they would go—TO THE BEACH, for, like, their first time out of the house since the Spring Thaw—and park their toad-belly selves out there on the blinding white sand in the blistering hot sun and they would stay there, nearly naked, all day long—and they would continually be SURPRISED to later discover that they had head-to-toe, back-to-front third-degree burns—even their scalps were blistered—and they would then spend the rest of their vacation time in the hotel room, covered in Solarcaine, watching television STANDING UP.

Nobody gave any thought whatsoever to AVOIDING the sun and/or attempting to perhaps temper somewhat its effects. White untannable people would, in desperation, slather their bodies with a vile substance known as QT—for "quick tan," I suppose, although "questionable taste" would have been more appropriate, since all it did was turn them a putrid shade of orange (plus it made them smell weird) and it was not even consistent—they looked like one of those hideous ombré T-shirts. I mean, really, is orange ombré really a better look for you than just plain white? The terminally white folks never seemed to be able to accept themselves as God made them—like typing paper—and they never seemed to give up. Whenever you saw one of them in the summer, they were Technicolored—either from their latest burn or their latest failed attempt at an even application of QT.

But anyway, even though some semblance of sun-SCREEN had been invented around 1938 (although only about a dozen different people lay claim to the invention at assorted times, so who knows?), I can't recall anybody actually buying or using anything that might create any sort of barrier between us and the fiery orb in the sky when I was young.

Oh, sure, there was sun-TAN lotion—but I can't recall ever having the funds for frittering on such an extravagance—not when you could buy a VAT of baby oil for less than a dollar. For just a few pennies more, you could also get a whole bottle of iodine, and if you added a few drops of that to your baby oil, the color of your tan would be immeasurably enriched—an unbeatable bargain that we all availed ourselves of, to be sure. It was not possible to get "too tan" in those days.

So, in the summertime, Caucasians were available in three colors: third-degree red (also came with raised blisters at no extra charge), ombré orange, or shades of brown that did not occur normally in the skin of humans, regardless of ethnicity.

We are no longer the Baby Boomers—we are the Raisin Generation and we are paying dearly for our decades of past solar indiscretions—we are collectively providing a most excellent living for all the plastic surgeons and dermatologists. Both male and female, come we to the surgical suite seeking to be hiked up, smoothed out, and excised, as the case may be.

Once you cross that line into geezerdom—and it seems to be a movable line—some cross it at thirty-five, some at sixty-five, some never cross it—they remain forever as they always were—some never age and we all know some folks who seem like they were never young to begin with—natural-born geezers. But whenever it happens in your own personal life—to your own personal body—you will discover that the words "high maintenance" take on a whole new meaning and that they no longer connote your being carried around on a little pillow by one or more significant others.

Once you officially become a geezer, you will find that there is some part of your body that heretofore had never required so much as a thought beyond the acknowledgment of its total cuteness, but now must be looked at or into, probed, x-rayed, scanned, irradiated, illuminated, felt, mashed, and/or filmed or photographed—once or twice every year for the rest of your life. All of these actions are performed by an array of different medical professionals, the offices of whom are guaranteed to be many miles away from you and from one another, have overcrowded waiting rooms populated with other geezers needing maintenance work, and are filled with copies of *Ladies' Home Journal* that were published shortly after the electric washing machine was invented. Your appointments will nearly always fall on days when the temperature is above 95 or below 20 and precipitation is likely in any event but convenient parking is not. Your deteriorating mental state will often cause you to go to your appointment on the wrong day entirely.

But no matter how inconvenient all this maintenance may admittedly be—it MUST be done and it must be done regularly. It is not necessary to do it without complaint—feel free to bitch and moan and whine all the while—just so long as you DO. IT.

Queen Robbiechey takes good care of herself and is quite regular with her maintenance. She has a home, home on the range, and I'm not sure about the deer and the antelope, but the YAKS are pretty playful in them parts. I don't think I have ever before in my life encountered anybody who raises yaks; you?

Anyway, Robbiechey and Mr. Robbiechey have a bunch of yaks—not sure if that would be a "herd" or a "gaggle" or a "clutch" or what exactly. I don't know WHY they have all these yaks, I'm sure there is an excellent reason, but whatever it is, it has nothing to do with this story, so fine, they're yak-herders—moving on. I'm not sure of the actual head count but suffice it to say that they have MANY, and even ONE of them takes up a whole lotta room, all by itself, as you may imagine. They don't even start OUT little, but I guess when you compare a brand-new one with an old one, the baby seems itty-bitty even though it's roughly the size of a riding lawn mower.

So, it seems that a new baby yak got birthed by a crabby or otherwise disturbed yak-mama who would have nothing to do with her newly produced offspring, and thus explains the presence of a baby yak in Robbiechey's kitchen, not to mention the dark circles under Robbiechey's pretty eyes—the result of keeping up with the very demanding round-the-clock mealtimes of the gargantuan baby who was named, for reasons known to many in the Queendom, "PrissyMae."

Robbiechey and Mr. Robbiechey had taken over motherhood responsibilities from other derelict yak-mamas in the past and they were pretty nonchalant about this one as well—at first. But PrissyMae proved to be a most troublesome tyke—the trouble being mainly because she was of unusual size and strength, even for a yak—and she was MOST insistent on being fed both promptly and copiously throughout the day. If they were the slightest bit sluggish in their delivery or if the bottle seemed to empty too quickly to suit PrissyMae—who does to this very day prefer large and well-filled bottles—they would be harshly reprimanded for their laxity by the repeated delivery of head-butts to their frontal regions.

If you've never been head-butted in the groin by a baby yak, well, you just don't know how motivating it can be, and it didn't take Robbiechey very long at all to develop a rapid-delivery system of nourishment for the bratty PrissyMae. (It should be noted that Mr. Robbiechey's frontal parts were far too tender and he was far too slow to adequately protect them from PrissyMae's relentless onslaughts, so the daunting job fell to Robbiechey alone.)

This had been going on for several weeks when it came time

for Robbiechey's Annual Hoo-Hoo Checkup and she dutifully kept her appointment. After her examination, the doctor came back into the room and asked her if there were any problems at home she needed to talk about, needed help with. Robbiechey was stunned—she adores Mr. Robbiechey and he her—no problems at home whatsoever—and this seemed like such an odd time to be asked such a question. She must have looked as stunned as she felt because the doctor looked very sympathetic and, dropping his voice a bit, he softly mentioned "the bruising."

"OH! THAT!" Robbiechey exclaimed, laughing. "PRISSY-MAE did that." As if THAT explained anything. The doctor's expression indicated that it did not, in fact, explain anything, and so she went on to say, "PrissyMae's my baby YAK." OOOH—now, THAT makes SENSE.

??????????

I suppose it's a toss-up as to who's worse about body mainte-nance—men or women. I do know women who've not had a Pap smear or a mammogram in a decade or longer—out of fear that "they will find something." Wouldn't let a gray hair go un-plucked or undyed, wouldn't allow the manicure/pedicure schedule to be disrupted—the OUTSIDE of their bodies re-ceives focused and constant care—while the INSIDE could be growing poisonous mushrooms for all they know—as long as it doesn't SHOW, it doesn't matter. When I encounter such a creature, I neither mince my words nor sugarcoat them—not even in the lexicon of polite Southern obfuscation is there any nice way to tell them they are STOO-PID.

But if I did an actual tally of the STOO-PID people I know in regard to health maintenance, I feel pretty confident that the count would be heavily weighted on the male side. MOST women DO go for regular checkups—guys, as a rule, won't go until something blows up or falls off in their hand. These same men exhibit an almost religious fervor in their determination to change the oil in their cars on a schedule set to an atomic clock. The tires are rotated and balanced with the same zeal. The slightest ding in a door is duly noted and seen to promptly and the tiniest ping in an engine warrants an emergency tow-in to the best mechanic within a five-hundred mile radius. In some cases, I've noticed that firearms are likewise maintained with loving attention.

But a physical? Just because "it's that time of year" and nothing is festering, swelling, gushing, oozing, throbbing, or hanging by a thread? On a likelihood par with wild monkeys flying out of their hindquarters—which, I suppose, might actually warrant a checkup—but only if there was a constant stream of them—a one-time occurrence would, immediately upon cessation, be dismissed as inconsequential and never mentioned again except as needed for a beer-driven display of one-upmanship with his buddies—as in, "Oh, yeah? Well, one time I had wild monkeys come flyin' outta MY ass . . ." and so on, as some sort of testament to his male stalwartness. (I can't believe spell-check didn't flag that word—do you suppose it really is one?)

Anyway, I DO know ONE guy who was somehow persuaded to get a full, comprehensive checkup—INCLUDING a visit to a dermatologist to have all his skin examined and explored, in search of any parts that might need to be removed. And it's not like he had big patches of skin that were molting or covered with sores or ANYTHING—he just WENT, voluntarily—because It's The Right Thing To Do. AND, even more unbelievably, he admitted it, in writing, to ME, and so, naturally, I am going to tell YOU all about it.

This is Jud's Story.

Once upon a time, a handsome young man named Jud went to see the dermatologist. Actually, that's a misstatement. He went to BE SEEN BY the dermatologist. That, in itself, is remarkable, but then it turned out that the doctor was a LADY and he didn't run or even slink off, never to return. He manned right on up and submitted himself to the VERY thorough examination. You may have noticed this on your own personal body, but in case you haven't let me tell you—there is SKIN EVERYWHERE and it ALL needs to be looked at—real close—because a Bad Thing can be ANYWHERE. This means that another person (the doctor) will be looking REAL CLOSE at ALL your skin—WITH THE LIGHTS ON. (In my current state of disrepair, I would prefer to have general anesthesia for this exam, but so far I have not found any physician willing to administer it so I just take a fistful of Xanax before I go and try to think about watermelon until it's over. For those of you who haven't read my earlier works, "thinking about watermelon" was my daddy's recommendation for surviving any Unpleasantness, social, spiritual, physical or medical—ridiculous but surprisingly effective.)

So anyway, Jud mans up and bares all and Lady Doctor she looks and she looks and SHE LOOKS, and by and by, she comes to his Down There parts and, lo and behold, she does one of those pause and "hmmm" things, right in the area of his Manhood—which he fondly refers to as his "ManWood," although if it had been entertaining any thoughts of becoming treelike under the circumstances, those were banished at the sound of that little "hmmm," as we might well imagine. It seems there was a Mole and it was, like, RIGHT THERE and it was the one time in its entire life that being the center of attention was somewhat less than appealing to his Manly Part.

"Has this always been here?" she asked, meaning, of course, the Mole, but all the Regular Stuff was just RIGHT THERE. "I don't know, I never noticed it before," he replied, also meaning the Mole. "I recommend we remove it," she said, meaning, once more, thankfully, the Mole. And he was told to return the following Monday for . . . THE PROCEDURE.

The fact that he DID return is a true and total testament to his über-manliness and I am so proud of him. A lesser man would have just left there and lied—until the mole and everything else just wiveled up and fell off. But, it must be said, he was not without trepidation. It must also be said that while one might THINK that he was nervous and concerned that the offending speck could turn out to be cancerous, but no—he was afraid he would get a hard-on during The Procedure.

That's all he could think about—what if I get a big boner right in the middle of The Procedure? And wouldn't you know it? Out of ALL the waiting rooms in ALL the world, HE has to be in the ONE that is NOT filled with forty-five-year-old *Ladies' Home Journal*s. No, indeed, everywhere he looked, there was nothing but *Cosmo*s and *Glamour*s and other girl-porn mags—and the cover of each and every one of them offered such informative articles as 50 FANTASTIC POSITIONS TO TRY IN BED AND ELSEWHERE! and MEN'S NEW SEXUAL NEEDS! and YOUR ORGASM GUARANTEED! and 7 BAD-GIRL BEDROOM MOVES YOU MUST MASTER! and PUT THE PORN ON! He's trying valiantly to avoid seeing those headlines and the nearly naked females displayed on every page—he's focused ALL his attention on a brochure with nothing but drawings and photographs of people with frown lines and wrinkles, entitled, Why You

Need Botox. This is helping him to remain both calm and limp until they finally call him into The Room, and what he sees there, while not particularly calming, does succeed in producing a heretofore unrivaled condition of Limp.

The Syringe. He walked over to it and addressed it, "Oh, my God." And although he now admits that it was a very tiny needle, at that moment it did take on railroad-spike proportions to him. As the nurse left the room, with instructions to undress and drape himself with the little paper blankie, she assured him that it would, in fact, All Be Over Soon.

After a discreet interval, the nurse reentered the room, made straight for The Syringe, and approached him with it. It was then discovered that Jud had failed to remove his underwear—which you would THINK could have been accomplished without specific instructions, given the location of the Mole and all. But anyway, after more undressing and redraping, the nurse once again stood over him with the sharp object and she asked him to please, ahhh, hold, ahhh, move, ahhh—I'm sure all the hemming and hawing was his and his alone; no doubt SHE very matter-of-factly and maturely asked him to shift his penis to one side so that she could give him the injection to numb the area. As he was relating this tale, I was thinking to myself that it was most humane and considerate of her not to just grab it herself and yank it to one side and jab him with the needle.

Although, as it turned out, what she DID was even more potentially damaging to his psyche. He's got his limp little guy protectively in his hand and the nurse and her needle are looming large, he can scarcely breathe, and, I'm sure in an absolutely good-hearted attempt to soothe his fears, she says, "JUST A LITTLE PRICK . . ." To which he replies, "That is just not right—that's just adding insult to injury." It took her a moment to realize what she had just said to him and then it was a long, long time before either one of them could quit laughing. I haven't quit just yet.

On the very same day, though, a good friend of Jud's was also going to visit a dermatologist. Now, what are the odds, I ask you, that TWO men who KNOW each other would be going for a "well-baby" checkup on the same day? I found that astonishing. Anyway, they ran into each other the day after their respective appointments and exchanged doctor stories—Jud's, of course, got belly laughs—the friend's experience was not so much fun. He was told that if his biopsy was normal, he'd get a card in the mail, and if it was not, he would get a phone call. He got a phone call. When he realized who was on the phone, friend said, "I HOPE you're calling to tell me you're out of cards!" and the answer was, "No, you have melanoma."

Now, the "good" news is that it was caught very, very early—BECAUSE HE WENT FOR A CHECKUP—and so his prognosis is excellent, but I hope what we ALL take away from this is that where your body is concerned—HIGH MAINTENANCE pays off.

Asset-Preserving Tip

Go for REGULAR checkups, you igmo. While it remains irrefutably true that Brown Fat DOES look way better than White Fat—melanoma does not look good in any color—so—use sunscreen, stay OUT of tanning beds, and you should know that self-tanner no longer smells funny, nor does it turn you orange, but you should also know that brown palms are not naturally occurring, no matter what your ethnicity—so don't forget to WASH YOUR HANDS.

~4~

Close Your Eyes and
I'll Kiss You

Okay, y'all know that, in my opinion, if you are under the age of forty, you are Larva—I find it amazing that you have all your hands and feet, even—that is how very "early" I know (from experience, personal and painful) your development to be. So, not long ago, a little Larva Queen wrote to me, all excited about her recent purchase of what she referred to affectionately as a "sex lamp."

According to her, this lamp shed ju-u-u-ust the right amount of light on The Subject, which I took to mean her own nekkidity for the viewing purposes of some significant other(s). Oh, my, that did take me back down—a very steamy road.

I can remember—very well, remarkably—the time in my life, so very long ago, when even broad daylight was no dampener for my ardor. I won't go so far as to say that my fearlessness extended to include fluorescent lighting—no human female form can stand up (or lie down, as it were) to THAT—but the brightest natural or even incandescent light gave me no pause, no second thoughts, before stripping down for a little slip 'n' slide.

There was even a time, after I discovered the gym, that I would say I was possibly a bit on the brazen side regarding the illumination of it all. Nor was it necessary for me to consider the effects of gravity—either on my ability to perform in any position(s) or, more important, on the appearance of any part of my person—from my face on down—to the other person involved who might have occasion to open his eyes during the performance and, as a result, SEE any part of my person.

I wrote the little Queen back and told her that I was tickled for her that she'd found herself that little sex lamp and I hoped she'd be putting it to good and regular use. For me and mine, though, we will be using that often tried and always true device that we have come to love and revere. That would be, of course, the sex DARK.

Undress for Success

If you are currently Larva, you are, as I have stated many times before, a Precious, Darlin' GIRL and you need to get as nearly naked as the law allows and run up and down the road—because, dear ones, I keep telling you, a CHANGE is gonna come.

Not only do you need to be well lit for lovemaking, you need to be outfitting yourself in a manner befitting your young and precious darlin'ness. The time for high-necked, long-sleeved, calf-length muumuus is coming soon enough. That time is coming for you EVEN IF you never gain a single ounce—your skin will simply beg to be camouflaged if not completely covered. Hardly anybody wants to see an old lady's thighs and/or bosoms.

I say hardly anybody because there are, of course, exceptions. Old MEN will want to see all your old lady parts, but ONLY IF there are no young parts in the vicinity for them to observe. So, if you are going to your thirtieth class reunion and you still look hot—by all means, go for it—within reason. I would say go right up to the very edge of the line—one side of which will make you enviable, the other side of which will make you pitiful. Given the choice, we will almost always pick envy over pity, yes?

One more caveat about even such a gathering guaranteed to garner a group of mostly geezers, like yourself: be certain that none of the guys from your class have recently cashed in their early-model wives on some newer sportfuck editions. I don't care how much of your precious darlin'ness you have managed to retain, the comparison will not be favorable. Much better to let him look ridiculous for showing up with Teen Angel than for you to look ridiculous for trying to look like her little sister.

A Brief Aside Regarding the Unfortunate Emulation of Youthful Fashions by Those No Longer Qualified

Those of us of a Certain Age will recall when Yardley cosmetics ruled the world and fashion model Jean Shrimpton was our Supreme Goddess. Twiggy was in that hierarchy somewhere— what a combo—and photographs from that era attest to the pandemic proportions of the worldwide outbreak of ugly.

Jean Shrimpton was, of course, stunningly gorgeous and she had impossibly stupendous hair as well—while Twiggy was just bizarre. She weighed about sixty-three pounds and most of that was eye makeup. Not a tit to her name, all knees and elbows, and she actually DREW on eyelashes with some early incarnation of the Sharpie—she had a total clown face.

One look they shared—and passed on to us, thanks to the cosmetic wizards at Yardley of London—was WHITE lipstick. Any and all colors of lipstick were frosted, at the very least, but the MOST popular shade was a pearlized white that looked good on NOBODY and yet—we ALL wore it. We were united in our desire and attempts to resemble corpses.

Okay, now, if you go back and look at photos from that time, of yourself, of anybody you knew—hell, go back and look at

Jean Shrimpton—EVERYBODY looked like crap in that lipstick. And remember, if you can, those few moms of friends—they might have been a few years younger than your own mom, but they were moms nonetheless—and they wore the white lipstick, too—do you remember how much WORSE they looked than we did in it—if such a thing is even possible? How can you look worse than dead?

Well, fast-forward to today, if you will, and consider the current style of nude lipstick—which is a misnomer because nobody has TAN lips. There is no ethnic group on the planet that I have ever seen whose members have lips that are the color of grocery sacks—it is simply NOT a naturally occurring lip color and it is HIDEOUS—on everybody. There is not a living soul, of any age, or any color, who looks BETTER with a little bit of beige on her lips.

A girl of fifteen to, say, midthirties can at least get away with it—they're pretty much gorgeous no matter what they do to themselves—but if you are over forty and you put that almond-colored crap on your mouth, it may well indicate to the world at large that you KNOW what the current fashion is—but you will LOOK like dog-doo in it.

And don't be ironing your hair, either. We did that already, remember? It was unattractive then—just as it is now—it will ruin your hair now, just as it did then—AND on top of everything, you will look silly.

While we're on the subject of self-humiliation—don't be

going out to where young people hang out and think that THEY think you are so cool. I promise you, they do NOT think you're cool. They think you are goofy and pathetic—if not downright gross. They are laughing and not even behind your back—they are laughing in your face—which you would realize if you put on your reading glasses. They will face-laugh at you all night until you get too close to them, in which case they can't get away from you fast enough. Unless, of course, you are buying the drinks, in which case they will be nicer to you but they are still laughing at you and being grossed out.

Anyway, I can remember my very favorite dress of one particular summer. I wore it while dancing with wild abandon in the nightclubs of Cozumel, Mexico. I learned recently that there are no longer any nightclubs in Cozumel. Well, there are still some on the grounds of the big resorts that have made their home outside of town on the beautiful island, but all of the ones on the main drag—the ones where my seester, Judy, and I frolicked, lo these many years ago—are gone. The cruise ships have killed them off.

The tourists who come in on the big ships are there for only a few hours during the day and the ones who come to stay in the big resorts never come in to town—so no need for anything downtown after dark. Sigh. Even Carlos 'n Charlie's closes at, like, ten PM now, for crying out loud.

But my favorite garment from the summer of 1985 was a black sundress that was up to here, cut down to there, and had no back at all until slightly below my waist. Lord have MERCY, that was a HOT dress! I'd be lying if I said I didn't miss the days of being able to wear a dress like that—but believe me, I KNOW they are GONE—goner than the discos of Cozumel. If I thought I had to try to squeeze into a dress like that today, I'd just hang myself with the spaghetti straps and consider it lucky if they'd go around my neck.

Suffice it to say, I took full advantage of my fleeting time in Larvadom—this was evident, even in my earliest incarnations as The Sweet Potato Queen. My very first Queenly Outfit was my sister Judy's 1964 prom dress. Judy at eighteen was somewhat more on the tiny side than I was at age thirty. Consequently, the dress would not zip all the way up, but I did not let that deter me in the slightest. I simply zipped it up to the waist, locked the zipper, and tucked the resulting flaps of the unzipped portion inside and VOYOLA! I had a backless green formal gown! Backless was a good look for me then—actually much better than frontless, truth be told.

I'll never forget what Raad Cawthon, hot newspaper columnist, said to me when he saw me in that dress. He said, "Damn, girl, you've got the most beautiful back in Hinds County." Which, to this day, is still one of my favorite compliments I've ever received.

Our first "O-fficial" SPQ Outfits also reflected my enthusiasm for age-appropriate nekkidity. They were heavily augmented swimsuits and they were, naturally, backless. Of course, the padded butts were so heavy, we had to wear tights and, even at that, be careful we didn't inadvertently moon the crowd, and the padded boobs were likewise likely to pull the straps off our shoulders, so we had to put a tie around the straps in the back to hold them up.

The next Outfits reflected our gradual move away from our fat-free youth and into the more mature garb befitting our Post-Larvahood status. The necks were high, there was some flesh revealed on our backs, but it was greatly reduced, and we wore the longest gloves available. They were not swimsuits but mini-dresses.

By and by, we found we could still get away with the basic design of these dresses, but they had somehow become shortened just from hanging in the storage closet. How this happened remained a mystery until someone (whose mutilated corpse was later found being eaten by rats in an abandoned Dairy Queen—the identity of the murderer[s] remains a mystery but the reason for the killing was, of course, immediately clear) suggested that perhaps it was not so much that the dresses had shrunk but that our recently acquired FAT was making them too short.

The message of the deceased could not be ignored (even though silenced) and so an arrangement of ruffles was contrived to lengthen the offending skirts sufficiently to conceal the excessive thighage. Before much more time had passed, however, it became necessary to take further action in the camouflage and concealment of our ever-burgeoning bodies. It was also getting to be time to increase the size of our augmentations considerably, since by this point we had gotten so fat, it no longer looked like we were augmented in any way. We just looked like fat girls whose dresses were too tight. This was not the look we were going for.

The current Outfits are e-normous. I insisted that the tits and asses for these suits be of sufficient size that no matter HOW FAT we ultimately get, our waistlines will appear waif-like in comparison. We are happily growing into them.

In acknowledgment of the painful fact that our Larvadom has long since been left trampled in the dirt and that we are actually, in fact, rapidly approaching Peri-Geezer status, the latest outfits reveal absolutely NO actual flesh. The nude-colored fabric of the upper portion of the dresses gives the ILLUSION of naked without the horrifying harsh REALITY of it.

The swimsuits of my Larva years were shockingly tiny for the times. Today, of course, they'd be considered granny panties, but nonetheless, a great deal of my personal square footage was displayed in those suits. However, even if I woke up tomorrow and found I'd turned into a twenty-one-year-old "10," I can't imagine that I'd go out in public in a thong. I don't care how cute your behind is, I don't want to see all of it and I don't think I'm alone in this.

Today, I'm not so much interested in going to a nude beach—I would love to find a BLIND one, though.

Asset-Preserving Tip

Everybody's always pretending to be something they're not. When you're thirteen, you're always trying to make people think you're eighteen (Note: Girls can occasionally get away with this—so if you're a guy—beware—be very ware—because you can end up in prison being called "Darlene.") When you're eighteen you want people to believe you are twenty-one. Then, when you close in on thirty, you start lying in the OTHER direction.

So much simpler to just BE what we happen to BE, in my opinion. Lying, about anything, is just too tedious to fool with—too much to remember. I knew a woman once who assiduously avoided any discussion of age—it was hilarious to observe the conversational gymnastics she would employ to steer the conversation away from that area—about ANYTHING. Any conversation that had the word *age* in it—you could be discussing wine, cheese, cars—any OLD thing and she would visibly blanch and create some sort of diversion—lest the talk turn somehow to PERSONAL ages.

She had a date once with a man who most of US KNEW for a fact was a whole big lot younger than she—evidently he was not certain but he was certainly curious. I mean, it's only natural, I think, for people to WANT desperately to KNOW WHATEVER it is that you're trying so desperately to keep a SECRET. Most of the time it's stuff nobody would give a thought to, much less a shit about, until they find out that YOU don't want them to know—and then they will go to all manner of trouble just to find out what your piddly-ass, little, insignificant secret is.

Anyway, he was entertaining himself watching her change the subject whenever the word *age* came up in a sentence, and while he grudgingly admired her ability to dodge and weave, he nonetheless became more and more determined to get to the truth. After hours, over cocktails, dinner, and more cocktails, either she was too tired to tango or he was too light on his conversational toes, but he tripped her up at last.

He casually asked her if she remembered where she was when John F. Kennedy was shot.

Just tell the truth—humiliation is, well, humiliating and, as such, best avoided. I'm sure it causes crow's-feet.

∽5∽

Tiny Woman Repents, Vows to Eat Cheese, Pies

As most of you probably already know, I answer all my own e-mails—love getting them from y'all, love writing back— but I got one this morning that I swear I will frame and hang on my office wall until the end of my days. It will make me happy every time I read it, which I will do several times daily, I'm sure.

Queen L wrote to confess that she had been brought to the painful realization that she was utterly failing at living up to the Sweet Potato Queen Standard of Living and, oh, she was suffering mightily from that shortcoming.

The first problem area, she felt, was her part-time work as a personal trainer, which was causing her to work out vigorously every day of her life. Although she swore she was consuming foods from both the Sweet and the Salty groups, as a vegetarian, she avoided altogether the Frieds and Au Gratins.

Okay, now I'm paying attention to her but I'm thinking the whole time that I myownself have BEEN a personal trainer and I know perfectly well that it is totally possible to instruct the CLIENT in correct form and what not—without exerting onesownself in the slightest, if one was of a mind to, as I frequently was. And since when does being a vegetarian preclude Fried? Hello? Tempura veggies? And why no cheese? Who can resist the Laughing Cow? She's so happy about her cheese and all—always makes ME wanna join in.

But anyway, Queen L went on to say that, as a vegetarian, her fiber intake level was nearly perfect, of which she was dangerously proud, if you ask me—AND that her "tight little butt" fit oh, so nicely into her SIZE 2 SHORTS. "For years now, I have been under the false illusion that all of this was a thing to be proud of." Her words, certainly not mine, as you should well know.

Size 2, my hind leg. Oh, she was a proud one, all right—and you KNOW what They say about pride—and where it comes, in relation to destruction. Uh-huh. Little Miss Tiny 2 done been struck down and laid low by a BAD case of hemorrhoids. (My tendency would naturally be to put whatever her affliction was in ALL CAPS, for emphasis, but that particular word is just so creepy to me, I couldn't bring myself to do it. I'm sure you agree.)

Anyway, her Problem was apparently severe enough to warrant a visit to the doctor—perish THAT thought; I cannot think of anything MORE undignified, nor, I'm sure, can she, which tells us this was BAD because she did willingly take her tiny hiney in there and submitted it to the revolting examination. The doctor pointed out that "although her water, fiber, weight, and exercise frequency were IDEAL (which she did love hearing), he went on to indicate that she was probably aggravating the veins in her leetle bitty rectum (file that one with hemorrhoid) by too much heavy lifting and too many squats.

PLUS, she was sitting up too straight.

Okay. Bless her heart, even if it is a size 2. She has just been told that everything she'd been working her butt literally OFF for was what was causing her such major grief in her nether regions. She was obviously shattered by the experience and I can certainly sympathize with a dash of empathy. After all, I have, with great frequency and a fair amount of regularity, been told that everything I was doing was wrong—just not ever, specifically, that I was exercising too much and not eating enough fat.

The doctor advised her to alter her perfect posture in such a way as to kind of tuck her itsy-bitsy butt cheeks under her a bit, so as to sort of "push" the little roids back up in yonder. To her horror, she discovered that, due to the inordinate number of squats she had been performing weekly, what passed for "butt cheeks" on the reverse side of her size 2 body were too small and too tight to be "tucked" anywhere.

whole nine and a half lines with which to convey other equally important facts about herself to anyone who might come across her in a coma or other distressful situation.

So far, on her bracelet, she has "Queen S. Diabetic. Crazy Funny. Really Cool. Always up for a Good Time. NOT FAKING—I'M SICK! Clean Undies on When I Started out Today. Get Me a Private Room. Don't Just Stand There—PRAY FOR ME!"

But she still has a little room so she's thinking of adding "Leave My Jewelry and Makeup On." Her children, of course, think she is insane and also trying to boss the medical team, even if she happens to be unconscious. I fail to grasp their point.

Queen S just wants the EMTs to know her feelings about certain pertinent issues, in the event that she is temporarily incapable of communicating those feelings verbally. And also, if possible, through that illuminating peek into her heart and mind, to inspire the health-care workers to treat her as they would their very own crazy mama.

6

Howdy, Sports Fans

A gaggle of us used to loudly occupy the third-base bleachers
on hot summer afternoons at Smith-Wills Stadium for the
old Jackson Mets baseball games—back when Mookie Wilson
and Keith Bodie were on our team. Afternoon baseball games
met many of our needs then. We could get some sun—which
helped us in the furtherance of our quest for golden-brown de-
liciousness. We could drink beer and eat crap—always entertaining for reasons obvious to like-minded individuals. We could
go to the bathroom and/or concession stands at will and often
without fear of "missing something" in the game itself. (Baseball
is so slow, you can literally leave for hours at a stretch and pick it
right back up where you left off upon your return. Baseball is like
a soap opera for guys—they can walk away from it for twenty
years then turn it back on and be totally caught up in one episode.) And, of course, there were the hot guys.

All the guys were hot, of course; it was summer in Mississippi—everybody was hot—but some of them were also "hot." Some of them were on the field, some of them were in the stands, usually not too far from us—because, due to our golden-brown-and-delicious imperative, we were most often scantily clad, which upped our curb appeal considerably.

The guys in the stands would sometimes pretend to be actually watching the game, and when they did, they would frequently, as guys are wont to do, holler at the other guys—the ones who were out there actually PLAYING the game—an assortment of somewhat predictable phrases designed to advise, encourage, inflame, and/or belittle and otherwise denigrate them publicly.

One of the most oft-used buzzwords was "GOOD EYE!" which would be shouted at the batter when he would decline to swing at a particular pitch, deemed by my esteemed and usually inebriated male colleagues to be "crap." Occasionally, the umpire would concur with this evaluation and indicate his agreement by signaling "Ball." This concordance with the ump was rare, of course, because for some reason, if one is at all convinced by the plethora of epithets customarily hurled at them by even the most normally mild-mannered of fans, the world of baseball has apparently become a safe haven and source of steady employment for scurrilous, underhanded, dim-witted, and, oddly enough, severely visually impaired individuals who have somehow become immovably embedded in the infrastructure of the game on a worldwide level and have, for reasons best known to themselves, dedicated their very lives to Ruining the Game for Everybody Else—so anytime the ratbastard ump would happen to make a call with which the beer-soaked gang agreed, such a rare call would bring forth a frenzy of "GOOD EYEs!" for him, too, but he would ignore them, just as he most often did the tremendous volume of less-than-complimentary taunts flung his way during the course of a normal game.

We, the female contingent of the third-base bleacher bums, had not spent the preceding years of our respective youths playing or watching endless hours of baseball, so we weren't really up on all the lingo associated with the game. There were, of course, the occasional Moms with Sons over there in the good seats (the ones with backs) behind home plate. As part of the penalty for having produced more penis-bearing people for the planet, for many years their lives had been not so much more than just so many interminable chains of T-ball, Little League, and whatever comes after that, so THEY HAD spent many, many endless hours watching baseball, and thus they were likely to be quite conversant in the lexicon of the game, but we were still young, childless, and blissfully ignorant of, well, pretty much everything. Baseball and all its culture was only one small and comparatively unimportant entry on the very long list of shit we didn't know diddly about.

But we have never been accused of allowing our state of being uninformed on a particular subject to interfere with our enthusiasm for it, especially if it in any way involved hot guys. We were there, soaking up rays, refreshing summer beverages, and admiring glances—we were happy, we knew it, and we clapped our hands. But we were also anxious to participate verbally whenever possible even though we weren't quite sure what sapient contributions we should shout or when the appropriate time for such cheers and jeers might occur. We instinctively knew that "BINGO!" while admittedly one of our very favorite words to yell in any crowd, would not serve us well in this environment.

We made a cursory attempt at correlating, in our minds, the various incomprehensible phrases our guy friends were yelling with the events that were unfolding on the field before us at a snail's pace, but we soon lost interest since it clearly was not about US in any remote way. But we heard the "good eye" thing so many times during this one particularly boring game, it caught our attention, and so whenever we heard it, we would focus our gaze intently on the player at whom it seemed to be directed, in order to make our own eye-assessment of the individual.

It didn't take us but a second to determine that from our vantage point in the third-base bleachers, one could not actually SEE the EYES of anybody on the field, player or otherwise, and so, until we could examine them closely for ourselves, we were not prepared to be hollering out our endorsement of them for all to hear.

During the course of coming to this conclusion, however, we did make a very important observation that I'm sure, once shared, will improve the viewing prospect for all future baseball games for women everywhere: some guys do manage to look really good in a baseball uniform. Mookie Wilson and Keith Bodie were two such guys. This seemingly small, but for us salient, point just changed the whole game for us.

With at least one of them destined to become a superstar of the game, they were immediately seen as stellar in our sight for reasons that had little to do with their admittedly outstanding performances regularly delivered during the course of the games. As a result of our newfound and heartfelt appreciation for their appearance in their little baseball outfits, we quickly worked out our own personal set of cheers reserved especially for these, our two favorite Mets.

"MOO-OO-OO-OOKIE! MOOKIE! MOOK! MOOK! MOOK!" was pretty fun to yell, no matter what he happened to be doing at the time. "Keith Bodie" did not exactly lend itself with the same phonetic ease as did "Mookie" to the creation of a catchy one-liner, but we did come up with one that made us, and, we like to think, him, happy as well. Whenever he came up to bat, we could be counted on for a rousing round of "HIT 'EM IN THE TEETH, KEITH!"

But our favorite all-purpose cheer—the one that we could, did, and still do enthusiastically employ whenever a qualified candidate pops up on the field—evolved out of that initial realization that there are, happily, some guys who do look hot in a baseball uniform.

Rhyming as it does with that one phrase so overworked by the guy part of the crowd, you can really feel free to let loose with it just about anytime during the course of the game, confident that the untrained guy-ears in your vicinity will not discern the difference between their shouts of "GOOD EYE!" and your own of "GOOD THIGHS!" It'll change how you feel about baseball, I promise. O-o-o-o-oh, hunny, YES, do take me out to that ball game!

Trolling

Sigh. At one time, that term meant that our jeans were tight ON PURPOSE and we LIKED 'em that way—wouldn't have 'em any OTHER way and they didn't seem at all uncomfortable, which is so incomprehensible now. It meant staying not just up but out until it was time for breakfast—and thinking it was just sooo much FUN. The only way we would do that today is if we were sitting by somebody's deathbed, and even so, it would have to be the deathbed of somebody we either liked a whole lot or from whom we anticipated inheriting a massive fortune—

which would, of course, qualify them for a top spot in the first category.

For some of us, it often meant smoking cigarettes, and for others, perhaps, on occasion, there was even the inhalation of assorted other combustibles. It almost always meant the consumption of adult beverages, even though it might be a few years until the law would consider us adults and decades before our mothers would. Occasionally, it meant that considerably more than the minimum daily requirement of alcohol would be consumed, but we were going to sleep all day the next day anyway so that hardly mattered.

I don't think DUIs were even invented until around 2003—you never heard of anybody getting a ticket much less hauled off to jail. (I can't imagine why it took so long for this law to be enforced—were they waiting to reach a certain body count or what?)

It definitely meant talking to strangers. This was actually our target demographic—I mean, why would we want to talk to people we already knew? We already KNEW them and had apparently rejected them—otherwise we would be out on a date with them instead of out trolling, right? Duh.

Trolling was pretty much a catchall word for going out to do as many things our mothers had told us repeatedly NOT to do as we could possibly squeeze into an evening. It is a wonder any of us are alive to testify to this. I am sure there are droves of Larva (persons under the age of forty) who are still out there actively engaging in at-risk behaviors—and they (not unlike us) think that the MAIN, if not the only, thing they are risking is the ire and/or heart health of their mamas. The ones who do survive (like us) will live to shudder at the memories of the risks they took—but that's many years and many risks away now.

For those of us who have survived the bankrupting of our youths, trolling has taken on a different meaning—although it, too, is not altogether danger-free. Today, it means our pants are baggy enough to be entirely comfy and they may even expose our knee-bags. It means, if we are wearing them at all, our shoes are like treasured old friends—no longer particularly attractive but delightful to be with, even for long periods of time.

For some, it could mean leaving the house BEFORE break-fast—but those are not my people. It does happen, I'm told, but I'm not around for it. Likewise, for some, it still involves high blood-alcohol ratios, but again, not for me, thank you very much. I haven't had a hangover in what, thirty years?—and don't feel the least bit nostalgic about any of 'em.

Since today's trolling timetable has been reversed, your excursion should involve a hat and massive amounts of sunscreen or soon your skin will look ju-u-u-st like those comfy shoes of yours. The chances of coming home with MULTIPLE KEEP-ERS are greatly enhanced today—because today, when we go trolling—we are fishing—like, for fish—in, say, the lake, for instance.

I myownself love to fish. I find the mindless repetitive hand motions to be very like those involved in smoking, which I never failed to enjoy, back in the day. I have never missed the way cigarettes made me feel but I have grieved the loss of all that hand-fiddling connected with the activity. Of course, it did make us look soooo grown up—in a way that fishing never will—but you do cross That Line with smoking.

You must know the one. You need to know the one before you settle comfortably into the addiction phase—which will cease to be comfy at all when quitting time comes. And of course, it MUST come. I'm not even talking about all the effects on your body, inside and out—first graders know this—it's not news to you. What I'm talking about is That Line. One day, you are a cute young thing, looking so faux-sophisticated with her ciggy, and BOOM!—the next day, you are "that old lady smoking."

Believe me, you will BE "that old lady smoking" to other (younger) people about twenty to twenty-five YEARS—BEFORE—YOU think you look the least bit old-ladyish.

But anyway, I find the rhythm of the constant hand motions of fishing to be quite soothing, and now that we live thirty feet away from a large lake, I can soothe myself at will. Well, I can actually indulge in this particular form of self-soothing only when either The Cutest Boy in the World or my neighbor Angie is at home. As much as I love to fish, I gotta tell you, there is a great divide between what's known as "fishing" and what's known as "catching." I need one or the other of them to be handy in case I should catch something—which is quite often actually—fish happen to like me. The reason I restrict my fishing to the times when Kyle and/or Angie can be quickly summoned to my side is that although I do love to fish and particularly to catch—SOMEBODY'S got to take 'em off the hook besides me.

Oh, I don't mind touching the fish, not at all—I even kiss all the ones I throw back, which is most of 'em. No tongue or anything, but I do give 'em a little peck on the lips. The fish I'm fine with, but somebody else has to free my fish on account of I cannot be trusted to NOT impale myself on even the simplest, most basic fishhook. My limitations are many, and I acknowledge them all—this is one of them—I've come to terms with it.

My other neighbor, Laura, is an equally large Girl when it comes to this so I don't feel too bad, but in a pinch, even me and my fellow wimp-ass, Laura, can be counted on to man up, which is a source of comfort to Kyle and Angie, I'm sure.

One afternoon, Angie and I were fishing from my seawall. Kyle was in New York for some forgotten and for the sake of this story unimportant reason and Laura was sitting on her own back porch, enjoying a little of what we call "Laura Fest," meaning she wasn't doing jack shit and she was loving it.

Simultaneously, Kyle called on my cell phone and Angie hooked something BIG. I was feigning interest in whatever Big News Kyle had called to share as I watched Angie's line being stripped out, miles at a time. There was something BIG on the end of that line.

Kyle nattered on for some minutes as I "uh-huhed" enough that he apparently thought I was (a) listening and/or (b) interested, until finally I could stand it no more. The whine of her reel as the line was stripping off was driving me wild. Angie looked at me and mouthed, "Net," meaning whatever it was, we were gonna need the net to land it.

Kyle was still blathering away about whatever it was—even though I had interrupted him fairly early in his monologue with the Important News that Angie had just hooked something big, but it didn't slow him down a bit. It must have been something he thought would really be of interest to me to continue in such a fashion. Shows how wrong he can be.

When I saw Angie's lips form the word *net,* I somewhat forcefully interjected, "Where's the net?" But he evidently thought whatever it was he was going on about was more important because he did not immediately respond to my urgent query about the location of the net. I found this irritating to the extreme and followed up with a much more forceful and considerably louder "THE NET! THE NET! WHERE'S THE FUCKIN' NET?!"

I didn't actually wait for his answer since I had just recalled where I had last seen the net and, flinging the phone—with Kyle on the other end—to the ground, I loped off in that direction. As I loped, I bellowed at Laura—in total violation of about a half dozen Laura Fest Regulations having to do with the at-all-cost avoidance of disturbing the peace of Laura during Laura

Fest—to get over here quick and bring her camera, Angie had hooked something big.

Loping back, net in hand, I could see Laura had loped her-ownself over with the camera and was watching, wide-eyed, as the line continued to strip off Angie's reel. What the fuck had she caught? Something big.

Kyle—and, as it turned out, our friends Allen and Jeffrey—were hanging on the phone line in New York, in total thrall regarding the little drama that was playing out on our seawall. We could hear them shouting but we had no time or inclination to respond, being in a pretty big thrall ourownselves.

Finally, the fish began to tire—but not much—that fish was not nearly as tired as, say, Angie. Her arms were about to break just from trying to keep the monster from yanking the rod, with her attached, into the lake after him. Gradually she worked him closer and closer to the bank. At this point, he still had not broken the surface—we had no idea what it was—or how big it was.

Finally, we could tell from the line that he was close—I was ready with the net, Laura was standing by with the Kodak on auto-focus. Angie had braced herself a few feet back from the edge of the seawall, fighting the fish. Laura was beside her and I was right on the edge with the net, peering into the water, straining for the first sight of Moby.

Suddenly, there he was—well, part of him. He was twisting and turning and his midsection broke the surface. What I saw was about a foot wide and about three feet long—and I knew there was plenty more fish on either end of what I saw. He was HUGE and I was broadcasting that fact loudly and with great excitement to the girls on the bank, the boys on the phone, and the world at large within the sound of my voice—which I figger was a good five-mile radius, easy.

The fish broke again and I saw that the hook was in the big fin on his back—he hadn't swallowed it at all—and so he wasn't coming up headfirst but kinda sideways. I knew he wasn't about to fit in that net sideways and I was gonna have to get down under one end of him to land him which I did and made the on-the-spot observation that there was no way in hell I could pick the sonofabitch up by myself, especially at that angle, without joining him in the water.

Laura was squealing—hell, we were all three squealing like big ole girls—and the boys in New York were pretty shrill theirownselves, truth be told. Laura flung the camera down by the phone and grabbed the rim of the net. Between the two of us, using all our strength, we managed to get him up out of the water, but he was too big and too unwieldy, we couldn't hold him, and we—me, Laura, and Orca—fell back in the grass.

We sat up and surveyed our quarry, with many "Holy shit's" accompanying. Laura recovered herself sufficiently to crawl out from under the leviathan and over to the camera. We could hear the boys yelling, "WHAT IS IT? WHAT IS IT? HOW

MUCH DOES IT WEIGH?" But we were too agog to answer them.

Our dog, Sostie, was right there with us—she loves it when we catch fish and she always races over the second she hears anybody's line tense up with a fish. Even Sostie was agog at this creature and she crept in for a close look. Now, Sostie weighs about fifty-five to sixty pounds—not exactly huge for a dog—but pretty outstanding for a fish. The photos show Sostie lying on the bank beside our Most Dangerous Catch—and the fish is bigger around than she is. The photos also show the fish lying next to my own extended legs—which are normally several hundred times longer than any fish we bring in. This guy was almost as long as my legs. You know I'm six-feet one, right?

Laughing fit to kill, we (Angie) unhooked the big galoot and we (all three of us) heaved him off the bank and back into the lake. It sounded like we'd all just done a simultaneous cannonball when he hit the water—the boys on the phone thought we'd been dragged to our deaths for sure.

I'm talking big fucking fish here. We couldn't pick him up to weigh him—and even if we could, our little scale is made for weighing your regulation-size bream and bass—its manufacturer was not really allowing for the possibility of snagging Nessie and wanting to weigh her.

We showed the photos to the lake manager the next day. He said he was pretty sure—if we had only been able to document it—we had the state record GRASS CARP. Bwahahahaha! We'da never caught the thing if Angie hadn't accidentally hooked his fin—they eat plants and are totally disinterested in bait of any kind.

Trolling report: Close as I ever got—or want to get—to a "three-way," but I'll share a big'un like that with Angie and Laura again any ole time!

Highly Personal Foul

Perhaps it's been a bit too long since I actually went to a stadium to watch a football game—the lure of comfy seating, a fully stocked bar, food at my fingertips, high-def screens, and handy (not to mention clean) restrooms have somehow triumphed over backless bleachers, warm beer, stale popcorn, and long lines for nasty ladies' rooms. Never been quite sure how the name "ladies' room" stuck—sure never looks like many "ladies" have been up in 'em—looks more like a gang of spotted-ass apes had been housed in there until their zoo quarters were made ready for 'em, right before game time.

And the high-definition thing—how is it possible to make stuff look BETTER on teevee than it actually does in person? So anyway, it's gotten pretty cushy to forgo the live experience at the stadium and so I suppose it's possible, likely even, that I have grown out of touch with the whole football experience.

This was never more clear to me than after the rehash of a Typical Game Weekend my daughter, Bailey, shared with me, during the course of which I have no doubt many salient points were glossed over, somehow omitted, or out-and-out lied about—but what was freely admitted to shocked me to my shoes.

My daughter is a junior at the University of Mississippi—Ole Miss—which is officially the #2 Party School in the EN-tire US of A. I have no earthly idea which one could be #1 and what all creates the distinction between the top slots. However, partying aside, she has made straight As since day 1 and she is on a full academic scholarship and I am pret-ty proud of her. Her father, whose enthusiasm at times is rivaled only by that of Eeyore, was inexplicably berating ME for some behavior he imagined SHE was engaging in, and in the course of his rant, he was also denigrating her academic accomplishment in a rare telephone conversation he and I were having about her. (It's not that it's rare that we talk about her—it's rare that we talk, period.) Basically, he was of the opinion that she was just fucking off and I was of the opinion that she was a straight-A student, and when I pointed that out to him, in her defense, he said, snidely, "Straight A's in PUBLIC school." That remark and tone, of course, just jumped all over my own personal snide button and I fired right back with a snappy "Well, it's the PUBLIC school YOU were kicked OUT of, buckwheat!" which did have the desired effect of shutting him the hell up. Tra-la-la!

People do have such incredibly SHORT memories, don't they, when it comes to judging the actions of their children as compared to crap they were doing when THEY were that age? I am amazed all the time, talking to my friends, my LIFELONG friends—people about whom I know MANY, MANY incriminating things—and they will be just UP in ARMS over some dinky-ass little infraction their teenager committed—stuff that did not even involve armed law enforcement or drug dogs or ANYTHING. And they are looking ME in the eye—right in the eye, without the decency of flinching or even looking the slightest bit sheepish, which they OUGHT to be doing, me knowing what all I know and all—and they are just going OFF in a big ole fit of indignation that, knowing what all I know and all, could hardly be called "righteous" by anybody's definition—about catching their teenager drinking a beer.

I don't think we're doing our children a service by holding them to a standard to which we ourselves never even aspired, let alone reached. And by that I certainly do not mean condoning bad or dangerous behaviors. What I do mean is that it is probably more valuable to our children to know that we are actual humans who have somehow managed to survive our MISTAKES—as opposed to holding ourselves up as the Standard of Perfection to Which They Should Aspire. They would probably listen to you more if you were honest about how bad you screwed up on occasions and what the consequences were—or could have been had you been as unfortunate as

THEY have just been to GET CAUGHT—which, truth be told now, is often the ONLY difference between them and you.

Of course, those of you out there who were and are, in fact, Perfect are in an entirely different position and I really cannot speak to your child-rearing dilemma. I am sure you are even more mystified than the rest of us that YOU have somehow managed to produce such a . . . TYPICAL child with such . . . NORMAL . . . ewww, dare we say it? FLAWS. My imperfect heart bleeds for you in an untidy manner.

Anyway, I was intending to talk about the fashionization of football at Ole Miss and I hijacked myself—what a surprise. Okay, for most of my life prior to the time that I actually had my own house with comfy furniture, big-ass TVs, a kitchen I could trash at will, and a refrigerator full of beer that I could legally purchase for myself, I did thoroughly enjoy going to football games in big stadiums.

I loved the whole deal of being outside with tens of thousands of people. I loved the communal hollering. I loved devising new and trickier ways to conceal large quantities of alcoholic beverages on my person. My seester, Judy, and I once carried a sack full of vodka-infused oranges into an LSU game and a Good Time WAS, in fact, Had By All. We even shared with a convivial old guy sitting next to us until he made the fatal mistake of cheering for the opposing team, after which we summarily cut him off, from both our stimulating conversation and our intoxicating groceries.

I particularly loved LSU games and also any game involving the SWAC—the Southwestern Athletic Conference, made up of the historically black universities in the South. Some of the best football players—as in Jerry Rice, Steve McNair, and, oh, what was his name again . . . Walter Payton—and CLEARLY, the best halftime entertainment ever in the history of anything anywhere. One problem posed by SWAC games, however, is that they are notoriously LONG. This is because, at a SWAC game, everybody is performing, including the referees.

The only time anybody notices a ref is when a flag is thrown—so there are LOTS AND LOTS of penalties in SWAC games. This tends to make the game drag out a bit, which is not a problem EXCEPT it means attendees have to plan accordingly for their game-related alcohol needs.

My friend Carlos and I set out for Memorial Stadium in Jackson, Mississippi, one fine Sunday afternoon to watch us a very fine football game. Carlos actually prefers *futbol* over football, but there weren't any soccer games happening that day so I won. We got nearly to the stadium before we realized we had no booze and no place to buy any. My friend Adrienne's house was right on the way so we whipped off the interstate and ran by her house and borrowed the only full bottle of liquor she had on hand, which happened to be a fifth of gin.

There were so many penalty flags thrown and so many vehement protests to them that, well, the game dragged a bit and we made the shocking discovery at *halftime* that we had already consumed our entire allotment of alcohol.

However, this is not a story about drinking but about fashion. Back in the Day, as they say, when I was going to the games outside instead of having them come to me inside, the attendees all dressed in what most normal people would consider to be appropriate attire for the event, which entailed going to a big concrete outdoor stadium to jump up and down and holler and eat crap and drink.

As you consider attending such an event, what types of clothing come readily to mind? If you're a NORMAL, RIGHT-THINKING ADULT—such as myself—you will no doubt think of comfy pants and comfy shoes—perhaps an assortment of just-in-case accessories, like a cap and jacket or some type of rain gear, no?

Would it EVER occur to you to leave your house, knowing that your destination was ostensibly to watch a football game— outside, in a football stadium—dressed in a chiffon spaghetti-strapped minidress and four-inch heels? Well, I am here to tell you that on any Saturday afternoon in September you can drive by Vaught-Hemingway Stadium in Oxford, Mississippi, and that is precisely what you will see on every female student in attendance. The ones not in attendance are at home sobbing because they didn't have a dress to wear that had not PREVI-OUSLY BEEN WORN and thus SEEN by all the other female students, who have photographic fashion memories and are immediately collectively aware and scornful of any hapless female who dares to show up on game day in a NOT new dress— and the shame and degradation of such a potentiality is so great, they cannot bear up under it and thus they remain closeted at home with only their false pride—and a giant bag of malted-milk balls—to keep them warm.

I do not know if this is a widespread phenomenon—so widespread that it could be called the Norm—today. Please e-mail me at hrhjill@sweetpotatoqueens.com and let me know if the girls at your favorite college have, in fact, gone wild and taken to wearing cocktail dresses to football games. I really want to know.

So, yes, at Ole Miss, they prance up and down the stadium steps in spike heels and slinky dresses—oh, but only until half-time. NOBODY stays for the SECOND half of a football game— what are you, nuts? By halftime, even their darlin' YOUNG feet are throbbing so much they can barely stand up and it will take some minutes to totter their way from the stadium over to THE GROVE—where all the partying is going on—and that is the Whole Point of the Day, after all.

The Grove is a beautiful part of the very lovely Ole Miss campus, and on game days, it is completely covered with the fanciest TENTS that can be had for any amount of money and/ or other valuable considerations, and the tents are full of large television sets, comfy seating arrangements, catered foodstuffs, and, of course, copious quantities of refreshing adult beverages. This luxurious array is, of course, paid for by the FORMER students of the university—these would be the current students' PARENTS—who are also out in full fashion force for the occasion—though cute as the outfits admittedly are, there are, thankfully, precious few four-inch heels in those ranks, which I think shows remarkable decorum and admirable restraint. I am told that the occasional mom gets shitfaced and dances with what most consider to be age-inappropriate abandon for that setting—but by and large, it's a pleasant way to pass an afternoon.

EXCEPT that the whole point, in my apparently stupid opinion, is not only to GO to a football game but to actually WATCH the GAME—and that, for me, would mean the ENTIRE game. I mean, if I was just gonna watch HALF the game, I'd wanna watch the LAST half, wouldn't you? At least know if we won and stuff like that—but I am apparently a dinosaur in my quaint notion of both attire for and insistence on observation of the game of football. For Bailey, football is just like the ice cream that serves as a mere vehicle for the most desired part of the dessert—the chocolate sauce. The game provides a convenient time and place for her and all her gorgeous counterparts to display their fabulosity.

They love it when they have a Manning-type team on the field—because, of course, that means more people in the stands (for the first half) to view THEM in all their finery. Sigh. And I know that, should I show up in Oxford one Saturday for a game, the daughter of that drink-dazed, Grove-dancing mom would likely not be fazed at all by that spectacle—because at least that mom would be dripping in designer-wear and cute, if somewhat sensible, shoes. But my own daughter would probably never be able to live down the mortification she would no doubt suffer at the sight of her own football fanatic mother—standing up, hollering her head off, wearing blue jeans and a Sweet Potato Queen T-shirt AND cap—Lord, probably those rhinestone sunglasses, too, if it's a sunny day—and tennis shoes—IN THE STANDS and WATCHING the WHOLE EN-tire GAME. Oh, the horror. I just love her too much to subject her to it.

Free Will Flying Leap

In my past—my long ago and far away past—life, I was a fitness trainer. Sigh. Those days are so very long gone. There are so many things I remember saying, out loud, back then, to clients and innocent bystanders alike in the weight room at my beloved YMCA. I firmly believed them to be true when I said them—and I must say that, IN THEORY, I suppose I still believe them today, although the firmness of my conviction has gone the way of the corresponding consistency of my muscle tone.

One statement that is outstanding in my mind at the moment, as I sit typing with my head flopped over to one side in an attempt to stretch the knot out of my shoulder—it will no doubt come even more to the forefront later, when I attempt to rise from my chair and must stand for a moment beside it, allowing the kinks in my hips and back to subside a bit before trying to locomote to a different room. I think sometimes that if the house suddenly erupted into flames, I would more than likely be charcoal before I loosened up enough to approximate even so much as a slow trot toward escaping.

The thing that I used to say, and there is and was apparently supporting evidence in favor of it—although, as I said, it is less and less meaningful to me personally—is: there should be no real difference between what we, as human types, are capable of doing physically at age twenty-five and age fifty-five. And I would say that I wholeheartedly agreed with that and was living proof of it myownself, up until around age forty-three—which seems to be the age at which I boarded the downhill slide, and I have never really gotten off it.

Now, at fifty-five, I can still sort of remember stuff I used to be able to do without thinking—walk ten miles or more in a day, curl thirty-pound dumbbells with each arm, squat 135 pounds, move stoves, etc., and now my iron skillet is a challenging lift and I worry about house fires a lot.

At age forty-three, the time I religiously allotted for exercise began to dwindle. The demands of single-motherhood, taking care of my own mom, running a home alone, working eight or more hours a day, AND writing began to chip away at my time for myself. Handling all of my other responsibilities—for which there was literally no one else to whom I could turn for any help whatsoever, it was all me or nobody—made it more and more impossible for me to exercise for an hour or so a day.

By the time I was forty-six, "my" time had completely escaped me and I have yet to recapture it. So now, at fifty-five, I know, without a glimmer of a doubt, I absolutely positively CANNOT DO many of the things that I could do at twenty-five. I can still breathe—that's about the only one I've held on to. And I wonder—is it possible to reclaim myself? What's the best I could hope for? If not twenty-five, then is even forty-three a possibility?

The good thing—and the bad thing—is I KNOW it IS possible. I have seen it done.

I used to write a humorous fitness column for our state's largest newspaper, the *Clarion-Ledger,* and during that time, I chanced upon the Senior Olympics, for which, let it be duly noted, I AM NOW QUALIFIED, along with AARP.

In writing about the Senior Olympics at that time, I encountered a woman who, at sixty-eight, after an entire lifetime of quiet and sedentary living, had become the leading long jumper in her class. I asked her HOW this came to be. I was impressed—very impressed—even though I was only about forty-one or so and at what I considered the top of my own personal game, and so sixty-eight still seemed ancient and remote to me—which it so does NOT today. Anyway, I asked her about her path to Senior Olympic gold and she said, oh, when she was about sixty-six or so, she read about the Senior Olympics—in particular, the long jump event—in the paper—the very same one that I wrote for—and she thought to herself, huh, I bet I could do that, and she just went out in the backyard—and started jumping.

That was it. She read a short piece about it and caught a little spark from it, believed she could do as well as anybody else at it, went out in the backyard, and commenced trundling herself across the yard in one direction, ending with as much of a leap as she could muster, then turning around and doing it in the other direction.

After a month or so, she decided she was making progress, and she was committed to her goal of at least entering the Senior Olympics the following year, so she dug herself a sand pit to land in. Just got her a shovel at the Ace Hardware store and started digging in the rock-hard July Mississippi dirt in her backyard. She dug it all herself then she ordered up a load of sand and she spread it all in her hand-dug pit herveryownself, Little Red Hen that she was. She wisely placed the pit in the center of her yard, so she could run from one side, jump, then haul herself up and trot to the other end of the yard, turn around, and head back to the pit for another full-body fling, so efficient.

She never said a word to a soul about it. She had a tall privacy fence around her backyard and I can only imagine that not a few neighbors wondered what was going on back there—if any sounds of her exertions were escaping the confines of her yard. The folks who delivered the load of sand might have caught a glimpse of what appeared to be the site for quite a large sandbox in the center of the backyard of a retiree with no grandchildren and their curiosity must surely have been piqued.

The postman might have been given pause when deliveries to her house changed from romance novels, candy, and old-lady clothing vendors to supplements and equipment for athletes. He never asked and she never told. She just kept right on jumping in solitude, and the next year she not only entered but gave quite a good showing in the state Senior Olympics. The following year, she went all the way to National and came home with gold.

It's only added probably a hundred or so good years to her life—plus all the men she meets are pretty perky as well. And it all started because she just got off her mature and matronly ass and TOOK, as they say, A FLYING LEAP.

So perhaps there is hope for even the likes of slack-ass me—maybe I will yet reclaim some vestige of my late, and much-lamented, lithe. But here's some great news for those of you Larva and even younger youngsters out there who are currently sitting on your collective asses: as you age, you will find that your capacity for THAT not only never diminishes but you will also, as an added benefit, find that you have EVEN MORE ass upon which to sit, every single year. Bonus!

Asset-Preserving Tip

Regular activity and friendly competition is supposed to be good for us, body and soul. We just need to find our special niche. Say, does anybody know if there is an Olympic FLOATING competition? On account of I am pretty sure I could start right in at the gold level of that one.

7

Fashion

Early in life I inexplicably formed and unreasonably held on to a well-defined ideal for what I would personally look like if and when I achieved Perfection. On that great gettin' up mornin', I would look in the mirror and grinning back at me would be the most dainty and delicate flower of femininity. (There would be only one person in the mirror—me—the aforementioned flower reflection would not be that of the tiny person standing next to me—although somehow, that's more how it's turned out in real life—but I get ahead of myself.)

The little blossom in the mirror would be, in fact, little—no more than five-two—and she would have long, thick, luxuriously radiant red hair—an emphatic auburn, more precisely—her eyes would be sparkling, twinkling, and luminous, and they would be green. Although diminutive in stature, she would nonetheless be built like a very small brick shithouse.

Before I Go Any Further

Let me pause a moment and say a word in defense of the brick-shithouse appellation. It has come to my attention that there is a faction out there (of, in my opinion, impossibly tight-assed literalists) who have decided, because they don't have enough to do, that the song "Brick House" is somehow "demeaning and degrading and derogatory" to women because of the "shithouse" analogy. Now, granted, lyrically, it's hardly a sonnet set to music, but please, give me a fucking BREAK. They have twisted it around in their irritating little minds to interpret it in a way that identifies women as "shit," and anybody with even the smallest fraction of a brain SHOULD be able to tell that it says nothing of the kind and they COULD discern this fact if they weren't so afflicted with cranio-rectal inversion syndrome (heads up their own asses).

These people have obviously never spent any amount of time in any locale where the only place to relieve themselves was right out there amongst the great outdoors. If they had, those individuals would have developed a deep and abiding re-spect and almost affection for even the most primitive of priv-ies where one could, in absence of actual comfort, at least enjoy a modicum of privacy in which to conduct one's bidness with-out worrying about peeing (or worse) on their feet or squatting on a cactus and such.

Rural dwellers considered themselves very fortunate indeed

when time and economics allowed for the construction of such a facility on their own premises. The pocketbooks of most families would usually allow for only the crudest of shacks for this purpose, and, while functional for a while, they were not generally as sturdy and well constructed as the houses—where the people lived—or even the barns—where the animals lived. In fact, it was not unusual to find barns that were in better condition than the homes—livestock and farm equipment being more expensive to replace than, say, people and furniture.

The outhouse was good for only one thing and nobody spent one second longer in it than absolutely necessitated by the moment's affairs, and so it got short shrift in both the construction and the maintenance departments and nobody much cared—UNTIL, of course, a brisk wind blew up and carried it off, and THEN, oh my, yes, then there was a great weeping and wailing and gnashing of teeth. Any outhouse was preferable to out-BACK and now they were forced to get back to nature in one of our least favorite ways.

Therefore, before the advent of indoor plumbing, for one to have an outhouse made of BRICK was the ultimate in the high (and dry) end of luxury, the most divinely decadent accommodation, the most conspicuous display of wealth and prosperity imaginable. Who, after all, had the time and/or money to dedicate to the construction of a brick shithouse?

If you had a brick outhouse (and I don't personally know of anybody who ever did, never having run in very high circles), you were, in fact, in today's nomenclature, THE SHIT. You could prolly be elected governor or even higher, should you aspire to such, just because of that brick shithouse, once word got around that you had one. (I've seen people elected on endorsements far less ringing.)

So for someone to be "built like a brick shithouse" indicates that this individual is ve-ry well put together, and this is a highly favorable and desirable compliment. This is not to be confused with someone perhaps saying that you are built like a "fireplug," which is an object equally substantial in nature but the comparison is not at all complimentary. However, brick shithouse is high praise and should you hear it applied in a description of your own person, you should allow yourself to receive it as such.

Thank Yew, Thank Yew Verra Much

A word about receiving compliments: there is a difference in HEARING a compliment and actually RECEIVING it. A beloved church-lady friend was paid a compliment by Queen Gwen, and upon hearing it the friend's face lit up as she tilted her head heavenward and lifted her hands. "Why, thank you—I am RE-CEIVING that!" A discussion ensued. Church Lady told Gwen that her pastor had talked about how it's wrong and even sinful to slough off a compliment with something negative— like, "Cute shoes!" "What, these old things?" That a compliment ain't nuthin' but a BLESSIN' and we should be GLAD about 'em and RECEIVE 'em as such. So now, if y'all happen to pay me or Gwen a compliment, we will grin a big thankee at you and tell you we are RECEIVIN' THAT! I encourage you to do the same—see if it doesn't give you and your praise-giver a little lift and a giggle.

Okay, so finally—back to the reflection that I wanted in my mirror—the elfin creature would have a brickshithousey quality to her and her little ole feet would be positively precious in their lilliputian-sized shoes. She would also be able to sing like the best one in the whole choir of angels, but you couldn't tell that just by looking at her in the mirror so we'll leave that for now.

Real Women's Fight Song

One more aside regarding musical references to women's anatomies that may or may not be construed as derogatory: in my humble opinion, as an actual woman with an actual enormous behind, Sir Mix-a-Lot, with his famous anthem "Baby Got Back," did more for the cause of Normal-Sized Women than anybody since Peter Paul Rubens painted that Normal-Sized Venus. It's one of the songs that I would like played at my funeral. I would also like Randy Newman's "Short People" but that's another subject for another time, perhaps in a few pages, I don't know, we'll see.

Of course, while I do think it's a positive thing for us to join in the celebration of our fabulous brickshithousey Amazon-ness and it's definitely a step in the right direction to have our large behinds lauded—won't it be a swell day for Womankind when the latest hit is "Baby Got BRAINS"?

My Failures Are Manifold

My sister, Judy, was six years older than me—she still is, of course, but it no longer represents the huge physiological differences it did when, say, I was seven and she was thirteen. Now, at fifty-six and sixty-two, we're both similarly geezerlike. But in my formative years, Judy's SHAPE created the earliest recorded envy in my soul. Judy's body had curves like an hourglass—mine was straight up and down. Other than the big disparity between the comparative width of my shoulders and the ostrichlike skinniness of my neck, my body was one long (and getting longer) stringy straight line.

Viewed from the side, Judy had parts that stuck out, top and bottom, front and back. Viewed from the side, I had a nose, albeit a small one. From the back, Judy's pedal pushers were pertly rounded, while it looked like a band of gypsies might have gone through the seat of my pants, so baggy were they, with no ass to fill them.

What I envied most on Judy's person, though, was the LINE across the front of her shirt. That's what it looked like to me—where her breasts pushed out the fabric of whatever she was wearing—it made a "line" and I had no line—I had nothing but a shirt full of uninterrupted flat. Topographically speaking, Judy was the Hill Country and I was the wretched Delta. (Flat land makes me crazy to this very day.)

Frenzied by Envy

I can remember trying on her bras back then—which naturally hung freely off my body as if I had donned a barrel. I would literally tie it in knots until I could make it touch my body and then I would stuff the cotton cups with what was probably the earliest form of primitive breast augmentation—toilet paper. There was no such thing as a padded bra then—it was strictly BYOB (boobs).

Bras were 100 percent cotton, straps and all. This meant one wrong move and your bra strap was gonna snap like a twig and one bosom was headed south. There was even a joke about it—based on a cigarette ad. Lucky Strike was a popular brand of cancer stick back then and on the side of the packs were the letters "LSMFT," which supposedly stood for "Lucky Strike Means Fine Tobacco." The not-exactly side-splitting joke was "Loose Strap Means Floppy Titty." It was a HUGE hit with the ten-year-old-boy circuit in 1962. Lemme tell you, they would bust a gut over it.

The cotton cups were made into their bizarre conical shape

by stitching that went round and round in concentric circles. I don't know how they came to select the cone as the shape—as long as I've lived, I have yet to see a cone-shaped tit, but that's what they were—cone-shaped. And even if you had actual tit-shaped tits to put in them, you ended up with a pointy profile.

I remember my grandmother—on Mama's side, of course—telling me that in the REAL "early days," a LADY wouldn't be caught DEAD in a bra—only a WHORE would go around "with herself all stuck out like that." It was simply "not done." Much more "ladylike" to go around with oneself all hanging down around one's waist, I suppose. All I can say is, Daddy's mama musta been considered QUITE a lady then, by those standards. I don't think she ever owned a bra, and if she did, she needed a serious consult with a Foundations Specialist.

Anyway, when I was prepubescent, there were only two options for grown-up underendowed women. They could either use toilet paper, as I said, or they could wear "falsies." Falsies were foam-rubber freestanding fake tits and they had nipples and everything. Oh, they weren't COLORED like nipples, just shaped like 'em. It was interesting to me that they made the falsies tit-shaped and not conical—indicating that at least SOMEbody in the industry knew what a tit was supposed to look like—but it sure did take 'em a LONG time to make bra cups that were actually shaped like the body parts intended to go in 'em. It's kinda like, what if they'd starting out making athletic supporters SQUARE or something, and then thirty or forty years later, somebody noticed that the male genitalia was not, in fact, cubical.

So Many Years, So Little Progress

After a time, somebody did finally invent the padded bra, but here again we find an instance of They Just Didn't Think It Through. The cups were pretty sturdy—more stiff like Styrofoam containers than mooshy in an authentic bosomy kind of way. Queen Sue was herself underendowed in the breastal region and she hailed the advent of the padded bra like it was, well, not the Second Coming because they had never come the first time in her experience; it was like Christmas came to her torso, and she was pret-ty excited about it. She was especially excited about her new one-piece blue-knit swimsuit with the built-in boob facsimiles.

She bought it especially to wear on a first date with a cute boy she met at junior college. They doubled with another couple and went to the beach for the day. They were lying on the sand, talking, doing a lot of deep staring into each other's eyes, and presently she somehow came to the realization that if and when she was to roll over onto her back, her new blue swimsuit ta-tas were gonna be all sunk in on account of there was nothing behind that swimsuit but your basic chest wall.

She didn't hear a word that boy said the rest of the afternoon;

all she could think about was her squashed make-believes and her crispy-fried back. Finally, the others all seemed to be distracted with something and she seized the opportunity to grab her beach cover-up and complete some kind of crawlin'-on-your-belly-like-a-rep-tile kinda maneuver whereby she successfully facilitated the concealment of the evidence of her fakery. Oh, how she wished for something to stuff that bra with.

I imagine that she briefly considered trying to writhe around and somehow surreptitiously scoop up sand with it, but, I further imagine, she wisely surmised that while the scooping itself might be accomplished on the sly, the wriggling motion necessary to the process would no doubt be widely noticed by and commented on by not just her own company but probably everyone else on the beach as well. And even if she managed to fill the cups with sand, there would have been the whole sands-through-the-hourglass effect as she sat up and they emptied of their own accord. It's best she didn't think of trying it.

There are, of course, many, many other augmentation techniques available to us today—from actual on-the-premises aftermarket installations to soft-shelled padded bras to the latest version of falsies—what Bailey calls "sticky boobs"—but as we shall soon see, they all pretty much migrate, same as the old-timey ones.

Sticky boobs come two ways—the first way, it's really just a strapless bra. The boobs are made of some kind of viscous rubbery substance and they are connected to each other in the front. You can stick these things to your body and they will stay there pretty much all day as long as you don't sweat much. One of the Queens—Tammy—thought sticky boobs were her ticket to braless freedom forevermore. Until we were working on the Parade float and she got hot and they fell out from under her sweatshirt and lay there quivering in the sawdust and glitter on the floor of George's barn. We didn't laugh TOO much. Far better for it to happen there than in her professional workplace—which, suffice it to say, is fairly public in nature. She's got enough to live down as it is.

The other incarnation of the sticky boob is not a whole lot unlike the old-time falsie. It's shaped a lot like it, nippleage included, but instead of the 1950s foam rubber, it's made of the same sticky, jiggly stuff as the strapless things. They do purport to stay put more reliably than the early foam varieties, which, I'm told, were wont to crawl out of their cotton cups and peek out of V-necks or sleeveless tops at inopportune moments. I have also heard this version of the sticky boob called a "chicken cutlet," which does little to enhance the mental picture of either the food or the breast it hopes to mimic.

At any rate, another Queen in a far-off land reported to me that she was in a jumping juke joint in a Caribbean vacation spot and the room was throbbing with the beat of that perennial club-fave "Hot, Hot, Hot." Which was just how she happened to be feeling, too—all decked out she was in full out-of-town-and-on-the-town suntanned, semiskanky slink with the mandatory mile-high heels, and she was just thinking she was SOOOOO HOT—dancin' and flirtin' and carryin' on, along with her girlfriends who were similarly browned, outfitted, and misbehavin' in grand vacation style, and by and by, as so often happens in these settings, the crowd broke out into a conga line and they willingly allowed themselves to be swept up in the "Hot, Hot, Hot" frenzy, and around and around the big barroom they cavorted with the Cuba Libre–crazed crowd. Presently, though, it being so much closer to the equator and all, a pretty good bead of sweat could be seen developing on all the dancers and prancers alike, but this did not quell the rum-soaked romp. Just as one of our revelers was throwing back her head to let fly a heartfelt "A-A-A-R-R-R-R-I-I-I-BA!"—her throat closed up and only a strangled "A-A-woolp" passed her lips and her face took on an ashen quality underneath her tan and semiskanky fancy-evening makeup job. This was because as she had simultaneously raised her arms over her head with an appropriate level of abandon to accompany her anticipated joyous cry, she felt a sudden slippery, slidey something slip past her nipple on its way out of her bra and the swooping neckline of her sweaty, semiskanky, slinky shirt. She felt it brush the hand that she had frantically lowered in a futile attempt to capture what had just made good its escape and saw it land in a shiny, sweaty, shimmering slide smack-dab in the middle of the strobe-lit disco floor. It was, of course, her chicken cutlet.

But the great thing is this: she and her girlfriends had INFINITELY more fun back at their fancy resort hotel room laughing till they nearly threw up over Little Missy's Flying Chicken Cutlet than they EVER woulda had if they'da gone home with any of the smarmy guys they were originally dressed to impress. And thirty years from now, God willing, they will STILL be enjoying that same episode from their suntanned, semiskanky, slinky, SILLY escapade. Time and money well spent.

Survivalist Supplementation

My very favorite form of fake-boob fluffery I have ever seen devised was shared with me by a precious, darlin' member of the Junior League of Tallahassee when I did my very first fundraiser for them. If you live in that area, do whatever you have to do to join that Junior League—those wimmin are FUN! It'll be worth working your ass off—which is the mainmost part of Leaguein' of course—just to get to hang out with them.

Anyway, at this particular event, I went in Full Queenly Regalia—which y'all know I just about don't EVER DO except for our very own Parade in Jackson, Mississippi, the third weekend of every March. But the chairs of this particular event had the great wisdom and forethought to make it a COSTUME-MANDATORY deal where everybody came dressed as the "Queen of Whatever They Chose," and if you don't already know this, lemme tell you, there is NOBODY more competitive than a Junior Leaguer.

There were evermore some OUTFITS up in that place that night. As I recall, it was slated to run from six PM to nine PM and when I left, at eleven PM, they were dancing on the tables. But, I digress. I was telling you about the best fake-tit job I ever heard about. This darlin' little Queen came dancing up to me and demanded that I feel her bosoms. There was no lascivious gleam in her eye so I did not imagine for one instant that she had any amorous intentions toward me whatsoever—I could tell right off this was going to be a valuable take-away lesson in . . . something. I obliged her and gave the proffered pair a pat, but she insisted on a squeeze so I squoze and looked at her quizzically, as if to say, "Okay, fine, now what?" And she, quick as a lizard, whipped one out with a gleeful squeal, "THEY'RE PEANUT BUTTER!" And danged if they weren't. She had two plastic sandwich bags filled with peanut butter and stuffed in her bra and that Peter Pan made for some of the most realistic falsies I believe I have ever seen—or felt.

And, she pointed out, if you for some reason become stranded and hungry somewhere on your way home of an evening—you could always eat 'em! How does one argue with such irrefutable logic? Why would one try?

Suffice it to say, I have failed utterly in these, my life's earliest and most coveted goals—five-two, long red hair, large breasts, little feet—none of that EVER materialized for me and

I am scarred and haunted by this abysmal "shortcoming" on my part. I grew taller and taller with every passing year—and only a very few years of that rendered me a total wipeout at any hope of being short. Sigh.

I'd have to say that my inability to shop in the petite section and wear size 6 shoes were clearly the most significant of all my physical failures because, after all, one can fake one's hair and eye color, and we've discussed at some length the myriad methods for building a bustline, but "tiny" is not a trick to be tried with any expectation of success. Extremely high heels do tend to make my feet look smaller, but that obviously serves only to compound the lack-of-shortness issue.

Bad New/Good News

When I was in the ninth grade at Peeples Junior High School in Jackson, Mississippi, education administrators across the land were struggling with two of the most crucial crises they had ever been faced with in the history of the American public school system. By this point in time, these issues that had already been plaguing big-city schools for some time had even trickled their way down to our own personal backwaters. School boards, principals, teachers, coaches, and even parents of students found themselves in a maelstrom that they were ill-prepared to comprehend, let alone control. And while they didn't devote any discernible time to the comprehension of these issues, oh Lord, how mightily they did fight to control them.

I'm not talking about Civil Rights issues—those were to surface soon enough, but those basic human liberties were mere trifles in comparison to this horrifying epidemic that threatened to claim and forever consign to hell the very soul of an entire generation. It's still hard even to think about what was happening in our country then, but I feel strongly that there are things that must be said in order to let the healing begin over this rift that has been a festering boil on the butt of our country for decades. Let us lance it now, with brave hearts, and walk together, without a limp, into the light.

Okay, I'm just gonna man up and name it here and I'll even confess my part in it—no pussyfootin' around—I freely offer here, for your viewing pleasure, the stain of guilt upon my own conscience. Bring your own dirty laundry on out here and we'll compare. The heart, mind, and psyche of every adolescent in the EN-tire country—even unto those in the very nether regions of Mississippi—had been infected with the same pestilence that had first swept with fast fury through the major metropolitan areas of the United States but, sparing no one, quickly came to us as well. Not since the horrific influenza epidemic of the twenties had the entire country been so immediately and inclusively engulfed in such a deadly plague.

Beatle haircuts and miniskirts had come into the world.

And they were—uh-huh—here, baby, there, mama, everywhere, daddy daddy—oh, yeah.

The direst threats thrown at us—in the most maniacal rants of the zealots with thundering voices and the very wildest of eyes—against the Demon Rock and his brother, the Devil Roll, had apparently all proved true. An entire generation—the hope for the Free World and the rest of it, too—had, to a person, climbed willingly, gleefully, into the big hand basket and hot-footed it for hell, and no amount of admonishing, yelling, grounding, and/or beating could stem this tide of determined delinquents.

For once my soaring height came in handy for something other than getting stuff off top shelves for short people in the grocery store. With my freakishly long legs and as-yet-unblemished thighs, I could fetchingly wear the very miniest skirts made. Of course, they were actually just regular skirts made to be mini on the mainstream population, which, from my lofty perspective, was mostly made up of minipeople—but hang one of those on MY hips and let the full length of MY legs unfurl beneath it and, well, there are a few traffic tie-ups in my past, I'm just sayin'. The very same legs that I had fumed and fretted over for their insistence on continued growth became the subject of photographs on more than one occasion when I dressed to reveal them while strolling through the French Quarter. It was a heady experience and my inner-hooker was unchained. From that day forward, I wanted to get as nearly naked as the law allowed and run up and down the road all the time. The law at the time did not allow for nearly enough nekkidity to suit me.

I was not alone in the felicitous discovery that I actually possessed an inner-hooker. Around 1965, everybody under the age of thirty seemed to have a similar startling revelation about themselves.

We soon found, though, that one's inner-hooker was/is not welcome in the halls of academia—it was especially unwelcome in the halls of my junior high school. Every schoolday morning would see a steady stream of students lined up in the halls outside the principal's office—dress-code offenders. We would be lining up to be measured—boys' hair and girls' hemlines. One could not come over the collar and the other could not come more than four inches above the kneecap. (There was never any mix-up as to which standard should be applied to which group.)

The Ironclad Rule of Measurement that applied to the girls at Peeples was four inches above the knee and this presented an insurmountable hurdle to me personally when it came to store-bought clothes. Everything on the ready-to-wear racks was geared toward the average-sized American female—and she was, it turned out, only about five feet four inches whereas I was, at that time, five-eleven and rising.

My elfin friend Cindy and I could shop together at her mama's downtown store, Freda K's, pick out the exact same skirt, and hers would have to be shortened to even come up to the 4-inch rule and mine would get me sent home to change. Only there wasn't anything to change INTO—there weren't any longer skirts to be bought at any price and we were not allowed to wear pants to school.

Fortunately, Mama was able to SOMEHOW—by sheer force of will and I'm sure not a little intimidation since she was also an Amazon and the principal was, well, he was SO NOT tall—negotiate for me a reverse hemline restriction that was based on a ratio of skin to skirt. I was allowed to show an equal PERCENTAGE of thigh compared to my more compact classmates.

This rule applied only to me and it did not create any rancor in the ranks since I was clearly, by a long shot, THE tallest person, male or female, in the EN-tire school—all three grades, the basketball team, and faculty included.

Bare Belly Versus Beer Belly

My legs were not the only inordinately long body parts I was given in lieu of the short ones I had specifically requisitioned from the Dispensary. My torso also turned out to be about a mile long. And the other fashion staple that made its first appearance on the teenager's wardrobe Must Have lists about the same time as the miniskirt was hip-hugger pants . . . and the midriff-length top—not usually in combination, though.

However, once upon a time, I had managed to go downtown shopping by myself with my own money. I can't recall exactly how either of these unusual circumstances came to be, but somehow, some way, that was the situation I found myself in, and, of course, no good was to come of it.

I went into a store called Vogue, where they had what I imagined to be the hautest of couture available for purchase in Jackson, Mississippi, and I guess I was feeling pret-ty haute right about then, being on my own shopping with my very own money and all. I sauntered in, feeling very sophisticated indeed, and graciously declined the salesgirl's offer of assistance, preferring to browse unmolested for a bit.

And then what to my covetous eye did appear but a two-piece outfit that I was quite certain Ann-Margret would wear—Annette Funicello would shoot herself first, Tuesday Weld and Hayley Mills might wear the top or the bottom—but never together, they'd never dare—and so I thought it perfect. They had only one in stock—it was in my size—and it was ON SALE—I could not believe my good fortune. I took it to the fitting room and, with hands trembling with excitement, removed whatever drab nun-suit Mama had made me wear and pulled on the top. I was not too surprised when it fit—I was fairly easy to fit on top—but it did fit perfectly. It was made of a cotton gauze fabric in a bright vertical-stripe pattern—a little busier than I would normally choose—but it had long, billowy sleeves, a low neck, a fitted bodice, AND it came to only about three inches below my bustline—omigosh—now, if only the PANTS would FIT!

Finding Pants That Fit has been my lifelong and mostly futile quest. I am always the wrong size at the wrong time. My daughter, Bailey, is the exact size today that I was waaaay back then—and she is, like, practically a SAMPLE size. She can walk into any store anywhere anytime and grab anything in a size 2 or 4 off the rack, put it on, and look like she just stepped off a runway.

When I was that size, they had not even INVENTED anything smaller than a 5, and a 5 was too big around and about nine yards too short, whatever it was. Those size 5s looked like they were made for third graders with tits.

Anyway, I'm in the Vogue dressing room and I've got on the FABULOUS striped-y midriff top and, positively quaking with hope and dread, I slowly stepped into the matching striped-y HIP-HUGGER pants—and I could not believe what my very own eyeballs were showing me—they fit as if my body had been painted in multicolored stripes and the paint had pooled on the floor around my feet. They were tighter than my actual skin—but in a good way—they were cut so low, they nearly showed my appendectomy scar—and they were even LONG enough to wear tall sandals with—this was an outfit straight out of *Tiger Beat* magazine. I could imagine Ann-Margret wearing this outfit on a casual date with Elvis after a long day on the set of *Viva Las Vegas*. I could imagine ME wearing this outfit . . . somewhere, sometime, with somebody—maybe one of Herman's Hermits or the Dave Clark Five.

Of course, I bought it.

I was so stupidly excited, I took it HOME and could not WAIT to try it ON for Mama. Wish I had a snapshot of THAT face. She didn't say a word though, just pressed her lips together REAL hard and did something she just almost NEVER did. She went and got Daddy. The reason she never did that was because, of course, he generally thought whatever Judy or I were doing was darlin', smart, and/or funny so he was not exactly what you'd call your Big Guns. This was one time he did not fail to back her up, though.

I was still in my room, preening before the mirror in my new skank suit, and he took one look at it and said in a voice I rarely if ever heard from him—very firm and very stern—"You are not going out of this house wearing that." And he walked away amid my banshee imitation.

I reasoned, pleaded, cajoled, and pitched all manner of fits, hissy and otherwise. I remember the pleading and cajoling and fit-pitching parts pretty clearly—I cannot for the life of me recall what my line of REASON was when I attempted to logically explain why I should be allowed to go out and about in my new hooker outfit—but whatever, none of it worked anyway. He was immovable—which also NEVER before happened that I can remember.

He did get fairly worn out with the subject after God knows how long—I was nothing if not relentless and finally he got up from wherever I had him corralled for the nag-fest and he went into his room and closed the door. That REALLY never happened—unless, you know . . .

I, of course, had gone into MY room and closed the door as well—with a good deal more volume—and proceeded to thrash and bang around in there just to let them know that I was still in the game. Presently, he called to me from behind his closed door and said he would make a deal with me that would allow me to actually go out in public in my ho-suit. (I don't recall what he actually called it but it meant pretty much the same thing for sure.)

Giddy and elated, I yanked open my door and rushed out into the hall and was dancing around like a little kid who needs to pee, anxious to make this deal, whatever it was, so I could get on out there and BE SEEN in my new duds. Still from behind his door, he said, "Okay, I'm gonna come out and the two of us will walk down the street together and if that seems okay to you, then I guess you can wear it wherever you want to." ALL RI-I-I-IGHT! COME ON OUT!

And the door slowly opened and there he stood. The sight is still seared irreparably into my retinas. He was standing there—in a sleeveless white skivvy shirt (now called a wife-beater) and it was stre-e-e-etched over his big ole belly and tucked firmly into a pair of TIGHTY-WHITIES. And he had on black nylon socks and FLIP-FLOPS.

I nearly aspirated my tongue. The man wore boxers—I never knew him to OWN a pair of those hideous white things—

and I've always thought that they are truly terrible things in general and on anybody—but to see them ON MY FATHER—oh, my eyes, my eyes! And the slippery socks—with the flip-flops—how could he even get flip-flops ON with socks?

He stood there just as calm and quiet while I peeled myself off the wall and tried to resuscitate myself, then he asked, "Well, are you ready to go?" And to this day, I wonder what he'da done if I'da said, "Yeah, sure."

Hiding in Plain Sight

The operative word in that subhead is *hiding*. I'm not sure that the current fashion trend of "full disclosure" or, more accurately, "full exposure," is altogether a good thing. In recent years, there has been a fashion trend involving skintight clothing that admittedly looks pretty fantastic on any lithe and lovely Larva, but unfortunately, way too many of us who do not fall into any of those three categories are becoming fashion victims and causing undue retinal damage to innocent onlookers.

My sisters, in this, as in so many other cases, Size Does Matter. And although I am all for Normal-Sized Women—meaning, I am so tired of 0s and 2s—really and truly, if we are NOT one of those, we have got no business wearing skintight garments out in public. Okay, I'll go as high as a 12—but only if you're over five feet seven. Whatever your size, there are no official body parts called "rolls" and/or "gobs." If we have those, they are not anatomically necessary nor are they part of the original equipment—they are add-on aftermarket accessories and they have no place in the inevitable spotlight that Lycra outfits put them in.

Fashion, although an entertaining diversion, is not mandatory, but I think a case could be made for any attempt at legislating good sense, if not good taste. Meaning that if one does not have a body that is in ANY WAY similar to the bodies a garment was designed for—one should not necessarily adopt that particular fashion. Just because they MAKE a tube top in size 3X does not behoove us to squeeze ourselves into it.

Although I have never been accused of being a "clothes-horse"—I'm much more of a "clothes roadkill"—even I am faced with occasions that require me to put on something besides my thirty-five-year-old Umbro shorts, Teva sandals, and a T-shirt— and I have found that there ARE garments that are reasonably current fashionwise that I can utilize to simultaneously flatter any good parts and conceal all the bad ones and none of them is skintight.

Here's a little something I use to guide my fashion choices: when I am so fat the SHEETS feel tight, I don't wear Lycra.

Okay, I Did Have at Least One Good Day

And thankfully, I have an unretouched photograph to prove it! Back before the earth cooled, when I worked out all the livelong day at the YMCA, I did have what most considered to be a Passable Body—even for all but the brightest daylight—say high noon in July—that direct overhead light can be most unflattering, right up there with fluorescent, although, of course NOTHING is QUITE THAT BAD. But anyway, once upon a time, a long, LONG time ago—I looked pretty okay.

And along about that time, somehow or other, I got a call from a Dee Gorton, a photographer who did a lot of freelance work for various and sundry national publications, and he was shooting something for *Health* magazine about various forms of exercise but he didn't want to give them anything traditional. He didn't want to shoot people working out in gyms or participating in classes in dance studios. Somebody had given him my name because I worked for the YMCA, exercised all the time, and was not thought of in any circles as "traditional."

I met with him and he showed me the one shot he had already done for the piece. It was about yoga and he shot my dear friends Janie and Neil Strickland—who were practicing yoga decades before anybody else around here had even heard of it—and a bunch of their trainees. It was a beautiful picture—all of the people were in either headstands or mountain pose, alternating, and it was set at dusk in the Ruins of Windsor—which was once the largest Greek Revival antebellum home in Mississippi. Thanks to a careless SMOKER—and really, THANKS A LOT—in 1890, it is now just twenty-three massive Corinthian columns, but it's ranked in a listing of the Best Places in the Country for Kissing—as long as you're not dating a SMOKER, of course—yuck—plus, if not for THEM, you could probably get a ROOM at Windsor and do a whole lot more than just kiss.

It was a gorgeous photograph and it gave me a sense of the way Dee wanted to speak to the subjects through his pictures— so for his depiction of "aerobics," I set him up with my Idols for All Time, the Golden Girls dance troupe of Alcorn University at Lorman, Mississippi. Most of y'all will remember that I have always felt it was an accident of birth—a cruel twist of fate— that I was robbed of my chance in this life to BE a Golden Girl— being, as I am, too old and too white—but that I did pattern our very first green sequined SPQ™ outfits after their gold ones and that they are and will ever be, in my opinion, some of THE. MOST. FABULOUS. Women to ever walk the earth.

Dee, however, never having been to a Southwestern Athletic Conference football game, had not the remotest hint of an idea as to what he was about to witness when the fourteen bronze beauties lined up in a sparkling array in front of his camera. Since the photo was intended to illustrate "aerobic exercise," Dee needed the girls to perform—he just had no clue what that actually MEANT. Music was needed, so I pulled my car up close to but out of the shot, opened all the doors, and prepared to crank up the tape deck. Wouldn't you know it—the only tape I had in the car was "Short Dick Man" by 20 Fingers. (If you were, like, twelve in the nineties and thus have never heard this snappy little tune, then, by all means, get thee to You-Tube and check it out. You may have to try several versions before you get the REAL one—there's a cleaned-up version where they just say "short short" man—keep trying till you find the real one and then try to NOT hum it for the rest of the day—impossible ear worm, sorry!)

I walked over and asked the lead dancer if they knew the song and/or minded dancing to it—she laughed and said yeah, they knew it—agreed with it—and would have NO problem dancing to it, so I sashayed over, hit play, and watched as Miss Lead Girl raised her right hand and gave them a four-count, at the end of which my field of vision erupted with the superhuman gyrations of the fourteen electrifying examples of pulchritude personified.

Thirty seconds later, Dee closed his gaping mouth and actually looked through his camera lens for the first time and began shooting the dazzling spectacle before him. The photo printed in the magazine was only one of the several thousand frames he came away with—it was an amazing shot of the Golden Girls, in perfect unison, just as they arched their backs on the backswing of a pelvic thrust that must have been measurable on the Richter scale—I'm certain Dee's heart stopped at least three times, maybe more, during the performance.

Then it was time to shoot the weight-lifting scene and Dee asked me if I would pick up some semiheavy stuff for him while he took photos and I said sure, why not—so off we go to his farm and off he goes into the woods and back he comes with this LOG, wanting to know if I can, in fact, lift it, which, as it turned out, I could, although, as it also turned out, there is a big difference between giving a big log a trial heave to determine its liftability and actually lifting it to my chest and then pressing it over my head and then holding it for what seemed like fifteen or twenty minutes while he made sure the light was right and then checked to see that there was no debris on my back and then shot a few frames—and doing all that over and over for a couple of hours in 100-degree heat. I could hardly hold the steering wheel to drive myself home.

But I did get a world-beater of a photo outta the deal, I must say. It ran in the magazine and a copy of it now hangs in my living room, albeit in a discreet corner of a narrow wall. Shot from behind, I am holding the big, giant log over my head and it appears that I am totally naked—which, I can assure you, I was NOT—except for my gold earrings, my weight-lifting gloves, and my nail polish. I look at that image of my muscles and my fat-free self and I shake my head in dismay at the very poor comparison to what I see in my mirror today. Soooo sad, so vewwy, vewwy sad. The first time my friend Liza saw the picture, she said that if she had one of herself that looked like that, she'da had it blown up to life size and it would be hanging at the top of her staircase, like the giant portrait of Scarlett O'Hara in *Gone With the Wind*. I told her if I still looked remotely like that, I would consider it, but under the current circumstances, people would wonder why I had a big, giant picture of a strange, nekkid, log-holding woman hanging in my house.

As I peruse what passed for splendor in my past as portrayed in this picture—it gives me pause and leads me to offer the following for your consideration.

Asset-Preserving Tip

It's important that you have a GOOD photo of yourself made at every stage of your life on account of you just never know what's around the corner. I'd almost go so far as to suggest that ANY TIME you happen to have a Good Hair Day that coincides with a Good Makeup Day and a Day You're Feeling Thin and are also Dressed Pretty Cute you should have a picture taken—just in case. Keep all the good photos of yourself in one easy-to-locate spot—in plain sight on the coffee table in the living room probably would be best—and give instructions to several people you trust COMPLETELY that, should you be suddenly and unexpectedly overtaken by Death, they are to go immediately to the Good Photo stack and choose from there the VERY BEST one to use with your obituary.

It does not matter if you haven't vaguely resembled that photo for the last twenty-five years—the best photo IS the best photo and, as such, is the appropriate one for your obituary. The remaining good photos may all be put into frames and displayed at your funeral—but of course, only if you are going to be cremated or feel totally confident that those trusted photo-selecting friends of yours can also be counted on to be certain that your casket remains closed at all times. You certainly don't want everybody standing around your poor dead, defenseless body making COMPARISONS between it and your formerly darlin' self depicted in the photos.

If, on the other hand, you still look extremely darlin' at the time of your death, THEN you WILL want your casket flung wide open and all the photos in juxtaposition with your lovely, albeit dead, face so that everybody will make those comparisons and be just pea-green with envy. You'll hardly even mind being dead under those circumstances—seems totally worth it to me.

Once again, though, it cannot be overstressed, those friends must be 100 percent trustworthy under any circumstances—even if you happen to die when y'all are in the middle of a tiff—you have to be able to rely fearlessly on their ability to rise above what was surely a petty trifle and do right by you in this, your hour of greatest and final need.

You might give them some degree of discretionary leeway about the open-casket thing. Say, for instance, you had just healed up perfectly from the best face-lift ever performed on a living human and your face is absolutely FLAWLESS but you hadn't quite gotten around to whipping the rest of yourself into a comparable condition of cute when you just upped and died. Your friends might then be allowed to present the good part for viewing while sealing off the rest of the crime scene—by ordering a special casket for you—one with a nice face hole at the top.

There Is No "MAN" in "MANPRIS"

For some unknowable reason, I recently read a fashion article about men's fashions—in a woman's magazine. It made references to "man sandals" and "man bags" and CAPRI PANTS FOR MEN, which are apparently called "manpris."

Excuse me—I can stand for some men to wear some sandals—depends on the guy, depends on the sandal—but it's a VERY fine line they walk in those open-toed shoes, in my opinion—assuming that you are like me in your preference for manly-looking men.

There is no such thing as a "man bag." It is a PURSE, and if the nicest thing you can think of to call me is "old-fashioned" for having that opinion, then I'll take it and whatever else you can dish out. If he's gonna carry a purse, then he can tote the Tampax and I'll leave my bag at home. I am just not interested in my man carrying a simple clutch, no matter how much it might complement his ensemble. First of all, my man won't be wearing an ensemble—if he is wearing one, he is somebody else's man—my mistake.

Then the whole "manpris" thing. I am SO sorry, but there is not a straight man alive who could NOT look ridiculous in a pair of Capri pants. Think of any even moderately masculine guy in the world—any of 'em—and then imagine him in a pair of Capri pants. You've just gone from Tom Brady to Ethel Mertz—no way around it. If you see a guy in Capri pants, please take his picture and e-mail it to me. We'll put him up in the Gallery at www.sweetpotatoqueens.com and start our own version of "Glamour Don'ts!" If you spot one carrying a purse, wearing sandals AND capris—you will win some kind of prize—but you can't stage it—it has to be a TRUE Sighting.

When I used to frequent the YMCA on a regular basis, my day started there at five in the A and M, not exactly the time of day when you necessarily want to see what are normally considered, in polite society, to be the private parts of any gentleman with whom you are not well acquainted to the point of extreme fondness. Right off, I can't actually think of WHAT time of day WOULD be conducive to your wanting to goon some strange guys' naughty bits, but for sure, five AM is just way too early for it.

Nonetheless, there was a man—an older, very tan man—who was an obsessively regular attendee at that time of day. For an older dude, Robert was in pretty fair shape, but, of course, not NEARLY as good as he IMAGINED he was when he got dressed every day for his workout. Come to think of it, out of all the fabulous-bodied men I have seen in my life—and I've seen me a few—I cannot think of a single ONE that would, in my opinion, look GOOD working out in a pair of women's under-

pants—even if they were, like Robert's, a nice shade
roon.

Where he found MAROON women's underpant
never know—perhaps he just bought the big white o
Rit'd 'em in the sink hisownself—but they absolutely
nylon women's underpants and he wore them—with a t
TUCKED IN—and SANDALS—into the weight room-
AM nearly every day of the world.

On the days that he DID NOT wear the maroon pan
wore a sky-blue tank-style short UNITARD and the ubi
sandals. Every couple of weeks or so, he would shun the
and the unitard in favor of a pair of white hot pants, also
very small tank top—and sandals.

The man did not appear to own a pair of athletic sho
I don't believe he had ever HEARD of an athletic SUPPO
The hot pants at least were snug—bwahahaha—they
"snug" like paint on a fender—but they did keep things
hemmed up, if you know what I mean. The panties and th
tard were most commodious and allowed for free movem
all the contents. But all of his outfits were at least three i
on the bad side of WAY too short. Thanks.

Along about the time that a bunch of us, men and wo
would be winding up our workout with some ab exercis
the big mat on the weight platform, Robert would arrive
his "warm-up" routine—which consisted of standing abou
feet away from us, with his back to us and doing some

scribable "exercise" that involved a whole LOT of bending over. There was simply nowhere in the room to look except at Robert's mostly naked behind. Helluva way to start the day, I gotta tell you.

In case you don't already know this—there is one always reliable way to discern—if you're really all THAT curious—whether someone has gotten that shoe-leather tan in a tanning bed. Get them to take off everything but their underwear and bend over right in front of you. If they've been in a tanning bed, their legs will be uniformly dark brown except for a horizontal white stripe right below each butt cheek. This is formed when one lies on one's back in the tanning bed and one's butt cheeks get mooshed down on the top of one's thighs—that little strip under there is hidden from the rays and remains blinding-white. So if you REALLY MUST KNOW, this is a fool-proof test—which does not, however, preclude its use BY fools.

We were NOT TRYING to avail ourselves of this information re: Robert and his mythic tan—we just failed, unfortunately, to go blind in time to avoid the proof displayed before us.

The Y staff was most solicitous of the members' likes and dislikes, wants and needs, regarding the facilities, staffing, and programs. To better hear from the membership in these matters, they installed a number of suggestion boxes in various locations around the building—one being the weight room. And so, SOMEBODY offered 'em a suggestion as follows:

Dear Y Staff,

We really love the Y and all the staff—the programs are great and we really love the weight room. There is a problem we would like to bring to your attention, however. It concerns a member who works out at about 5:30 a.m. every day. His name is Robert and he wears very short and revealing clothing for his workouts. The problem is this: we honestly feel that there ARE parts of Robert's ass and other stuff that we have NOT YET SEEN and we were wondering if you would mind addressing this omission with him as we feel certain that it is an inadvertent oversight on his part and that as soon as he is made AWARE of this deficiency, he will make all good haste to show us EVERYTHING and then we can finally relax.

Thank you for your prompt attention to this bothersome matter.

Some Early Birds

P.S.—We really love the maroon panties and think they should be the new uniform for the male members of the weight room and front desk staff.

S.E.B.

And for SOME reason, they thought I wrote it! Go figger.

Die, Girdle, Die!

The feminine fashion markets today are flooded with all manner of garments promising safe and effective girth control—at least for the hours of the day that we spend clothed—and they promise to do it invisibly and with no personal effort required of us, the intended victim, ahh, wearer of these magic garments.

I scoff and I do so with authority born of miserable, sweaty experience. Call it what you will, it's a GIRDLE and I have definitely been there and worn that.

Okay this is one of those we-walked-six-miles-in-the-snow-barefoot-to-school-every-day stories, only it's actually, horrifically TRUE: when I was in JUNIOR HIGH, we had to wear dresses and stockings to school EVERY DAY. Let me just tell you—unless you lived in the Time Before Pantyhose and Tampax, you don't know shit about misery.

I'm not going to dignify antiquated feminine hygiene products with any discussion at all and I am thinking of becoming Catholic for the sole purpose of nominating Dr. Earle Haas for sainthood—he invented tampons, bounteous blessings be upon him and all of his house forever and ever, amen. Somebody did officially name him as one of the "1000 Makers of the Twentieth Century." I trust he was at the very top of the list—and, in my opinion, Allen Gant, the pantyhose patriarch, should be right up there with him.

We had to wear stockings to school every single day and there was no such thing as pantyhose yet and garter belts, along with pierced ears, were for whores. We had to wear GIRDLES to keep our stockings up. This was because the huge Girdle Political Action Committee had successfully lobbied the World Fashion Powers and convinced THEM to convince US that "girdles were glamorous." What do you reckon THAT cost 'em? I'm thinking somebody's plastic surgery got fully funded on that little boondoggle.

Miserably tight and wretchedly hot, certainly two of my tip-top desires for clothing, the attached garters that were smashed into your flesh by the legs of the girdle were of particular interest to me because, as it turns out, I have a mild sensitivity to latex. "Mild" in that, as a sexually active adult, I would not be able to detect the presence of a latex condom, any more than I could detect a lit match—down there. This, of course, was back before "latex sensitivity" had been invented, though, so nobody knew why I would develop such painful lesions on my thighs from simply wearing stockings like everybody else.

It's almost inconceivable, some of the crap women have been persuaded to put upon their own persons over the years— and the girdle was just one more example. You gotta hand it to guys—they might be led for a time down the path of mullets and Moe-Dos, and okay, I'll grant you, the leisure suit was pretty awful—but you won't see THEM goaded into wearing girdles. (Unless we could convince them that, no, we didn't mean "girdles are hot" but "girdles are HOT"—in which case, they would all be racing out to get 'em and stuffing themselves into 'em, so fast as to induce head-spinning in casual observers, which, when you think about it, would be pretty entertaining, wouldn't it?)

I suppose the girdle was an improvement over the corset—but that seems a lot like saying it's better to get hit by a bus than to be thrown out of an airplane. It always seemed to me that if you had to wear stockings, a garter belt was at least a cooler way to keep them up—anything would be better than a rubber suit, seemed like to me—whores were looking smarter to me all the time. They pierced their ears so their earrings didn't pinch and they didn't sweat to death just to keep their hose hiked up—made sense to me.

Girdles were tight and hot and the garters made permanent indentations in your thighs—it's hard to imagine that it was possible to get women to willingly wear them, but, like every other female in the country between the ages of thirteen and a thousand, I fell victim to the dictates of *Vogue* magazine that, sooner or later, trickled down even unto the sweat-soaked, fashion-impaired hinterlands of Mississippi. And so it came to pass that I found myself weighing, at the most, including the girdle and my shoes, maybe 110 pounds—but it's 90 degrees inside our school (that was decades away from being air-conditioned, by the way) and, under my dress, I'm wearing a GIRDLE that is made of something called Lastex, which is rubber's second cousin, once removed, to keep my nylon stockings up. I am talking HOT and a disposition that could most charitably be described as "nasty." Is there anything on earth more ill than the temper of a woman in tight clothing on a hot day? Perhaps if a wolverine could be fitted with a girdle in July—that might come close.

Girdle manufacturers made a pretty commanding case for their product—claiming that women who wore girdles described themselves as "feeling more organized, more alert, more authoritative and attractive." I don't know that I could formulate a coherent response to those women. First of all, I don't know and can't imagine that those women actually existed or that they actually said those things, of their own free will, with no money OR drugs involved.

When PANTYHOSE came along, it was like a worldwide edict of "WOMAN—THOU ART LOOSED!" and I'm sure there were countless men who escaped wholesale slaughter every summer as a direct result of our dispositions being thusly improved.

Women were actually being slowly liberated—first from the corset by the girdle, then from the girdle by the pantyhose—true life-changing progress and only over the course of about fifty-some-odd years—astounding, in an evolutionary sense. Of course, for those of us who were LIVING THROUGH all this delightful progress, it was not unlike hell, if, like me, you think that one of its famed circles is a tight waistband on a hot day. But now, all that we have suffered for and gained is in jeopardy if not altogether lost.

Bare-Legged but Back in the Girdle?

I have no idea WHO in the pantyhose cartel pissed off the fashionistas to bring us all into the current state of mandated year-round bare-leggedness, but, lordinheaven, I will be so glad when this feud is over. Whoever you pantyhose people are out there—cough up whatever ransom the fashion freaks are demanding so they will declare once again that women's hosiery is de rigueur and the ugly can stop.

Oh, please. Summertime, in a sundress with sandals, of course, just please, not too-too short if you're over forty. But I don't care how young you are and how gorgeous your gams are—in the wintertime, the bets are not so much off as they are frozen. Goose bumps are not attractive—no matter how tender the age of the goose. Whatever the season, for a woman to be all dressed up and have her bare feet stuck in a pair of pumps—yuck—it looks like a guy in a tux with no socks on. And have you looked at what it does to the insides of your shoes? Even bigger yuck.

But now let's talk about your older, more mature stems—or tree trunks, as the case may be—and the bare-legged thing. Oh, it is bad. I don't want to hurt your feelings, but until hose make a comeback, you need to be wearing slacks. Sure, hunny, if your legs are good, you can still do sundresses and the like for casual wear. And I know you might be in great shape and therefore you might think you still look pretty snappy in your business attire and Ferragamos, but before you go out like that again, please, put on your reading glasses and gaze downward at the skin on your legs. THAT is what they look like to everybody in the entire world who's under forty—because THEY can actually SEE.

But now they have taken away our camouflage, sent us out with all our spider veins laid naked before the world, AND they've put us BACK in the GIRDLE! I don't care what cute name you market it under—it is a GIRDLE and I am agin it!

(Amusing aside regarding cute product names: No matter how cute and/or simple you try to make it—somebody somewhere will screw it up. I read a whole column of fashion tips in the newspaper once and the so-called consultant was recommending the Spanx brand of foundation garments—except he was an idiot and kept calling it The Spank. How hard is it to read a one-word label? But then I ran across a woman who had been advised by her "consultant" to get some Spanx, only she didn't know about 'em and apparently didn't understand the instructions because she called all her friends to report that she had been out all day trying to buy a SKANK and she could not wear this new dress until she got a SKANK and did we know where the hell you could buy a fucking SKANK in this town?

We were pretty tickled—and, of course, now WE call 'em Skanx.)

Back to the stream of consciousness: Not only is it positively torture to have to walk around in all day, a girdle is like the reverse equivalent of falsies—in that, sooner or later, the Truth WILL Out and it's not likely to win any beauty contests when it do. If you're flat, you're flat—if you're fat, you're fat—and no amount of supplementing or squeezing will fool anybody to the contrary for very long. The only true remedy for either condition must be permanent—in the form of either acceptance or actual change—or you're doomed to forever fooling with some uncomfortable contrivance.

I will admit that a panty with power—especially one with the power extended midway down one's thighs—can be advantageous if for no other reason than this: no matter what shape your shape is in, this foundation garment WILL smash your butt cheeks so firmly together that there is absolutely no danger of your outer garment becoming lodged between them, and that's a plus, I don't care who you are. For this achievement alone, the creator of them deserves the Nobel Prize for Engineering. And it should be noted that this would be THE ONLY benefit the model on the package could conceivably NEED from this product.

The problem with these squeezy suits is a natural by-product of the original positive intent for them. Unwitting pudgy people are duped into buying them because of our unwavering willingness to believe in the concept of The Immaculate Reduction. We view the photos of the models wearing the various miracle suits and we immediately, in our mind's eye, see ourselves svelte, like this model right here on this package. We want more than just about anything for there to be some instant fix for our fat—something work- and deprivation-free. Something to keep our thighs from sticking together in the summer like massive, sweaty flesh magnets. I'd give strong consideration to taking it over world peace if the two were offered up—but, of course, neither one of 'em is what you'd exactly call LIKELY.

But step back and allow yourself to SEE one of the models they use for these cruel ads. Were you to see her in real life, in person, in natural light, you would swear she had been chained to a radiator in an unlit basement and fed nothing but cellophane for the last eight years. And yet she looks lithe and lovely in the photograph—that's because, using the forensic computer technology developed for re-creating the faces of mummified remains, they air-brushed FLESH onto her bones for the photo.

You imagine that if she were to peel away the miraculous microfiber vestments, her true physique would unfurl and she would actually look a lot like, well, you. The Truth is this: what with the marvels of augmentation surgery available today, if we were to chance upon her in a state of full nekkidity, we would likely mistake her for a nightstand with the top drawer pulled out.

Matter is never lost in the entire Universe—this is why it is impossible for there to be an overall net weight loss among the human race. If one of us loses a pound, another one of us finds it, and so the weight just gets passed around unto infinity. If it cannot be lost, why are we so easily persuaded that it can at least be hidden?

If they hired a model from within the ranks of the actual living humans who regularly consumes calories—well, never mind—THAT is never going to happen. BECAUSE you know what happens when a genuine figure flaw is forced into Lycra: it just pops out somewhere else. The photo of a REAL woman in a pair of power panties might indeed render the square footage actually contained within them smooth and firm—but if you were to shift the camera at all, you would see fat stuff poking out all over the place. You wouldn't be able to actually SEE the waistband because it would be completely covered by the fat that was pushed up and out by the powerful panties—and having no vertical support, it just lops over the waistband and rests comfortably on the top of the hips.

My favorite are the swimsuits that offer "tummy control." Okay, these might be beneficial if your ONLY problem area is a very slight stomachular pooch. I don't know that I've ever encountered any woman who was perfect in every way, except for that one little bitty bulge below her belly button. Maybe you're her and if so, fine—get you one of these bathing suits or pairs of slacks or skintight dresses all currently in the marketplace that claim they will cause you to immediately look five pounds thinner if you put them on.

And can we just say that if a five-pound improvement is all you need—you really don't need ANYTHING, you skinny bitch, get away from me, you make me look even fatter.

But let's just say that you are, for the sake of discussion, NORMAL, and, as such, there is spare You everywhere—not just on your tummy but on your back and your arms and your butt and your thighs—just everydamnwhere—but let's just talk thighs here for a minute. See, the "control" stuff they use is not just across the tummy part—it's the whole bottom half of the suit—including, of course, the LEG HOLES, and what that means to you, if you have ANY bonus flesh on the upper portion of your legs, is it's going to look like you have, for reasons best known to yourself, chosen to come poolside with extremely tight rubber bands on the tops of your thighs and so to the horrified observer it will appear that you were going for the Pontoon Look today.

When you squeeze your fat it can go "in" only so far—on account of we have inconveniently located vital organs and bones in there taking up valuable fat storage space. Thus, the squozen fat mostly has to go either north or south and so you don't really so much eliminate bulges as you relocate them. The only possibility I can see for eliminating the Rubber Band Effect is to make Lycra long johns. Of course, even that is not without unwanted side effects, like swelling, and then your rings and shoes won't fit but at least you won't be lumpy. You might even notice your necklaces feeling snug, but if your glasses are feeling too tight, by all means go to a secure area and try to slowly open a safety valve somewhere in the suit to take the pressure off before gangrene sets in.

Thy Merrell Sandals and Thy Big Panties, They Comfort Me

I couldn't say with certainty when the line was crossed—I don't remember seeing it off in the distance, moving closer to it, and finally crossing it, leaving it fading farther and farther into the distance behind me as I move relentlessly forward on Life's Pathway. But I can tell you that on THIS side of that line, a chance meeting with a girlfriend is not likely to bring with it those squeals of "HEEEYYY! CUTE SHOES!" On account of we are both wearing Merrell sandals—usually black slides—they are indescribably comfy.

Seriously, I saw my friend Adrienne the other night for the first time in about five years—and she, at least, has always been a real fashion plate. I can't recall ever seeing her when she wasn't "put together." On my BEST day, those words would not describe me—I'm more often described as "clean," but only when people for some reason feel obligated to compliment me on SOMETHING. On this occasion, however, we both had on deliciously loose, sacklike cotton clothing and the same I-DENTICAL black Merrell slides and we actually did engage in a brief exchange of "Heeeyy! Cute shoes!" but you could tell it was hardly the same—black Merrells just don't evoke squealage from spectators. You'll hear some definite sincere moans of pleasure, however, in the shoe store when someone our age tries them on for the first time. And that's all it takes—your Cute Shoes days are over.

And the really great thing is—I know it's impossible for some of y'all to believe it right now, just trust me on this as you have come to do on so many other important life issues—you will NOT be sorry. In fact, you will wonderingly ponder on the fast-fading memories of the time in your life when you sought out shoes with three-inch heels to wear to work—because they were then perfect to wear straight to the dance floor, should you work overtime on your regular Thursday night session of red town-painting.

Hey—speaking of that—why would anybody want to paint a town—red or otherwise—and think that was a fun way to spend an evening? Just curious. Although, as I think about it, every house painter I personally have ever employed has been a religiously practicing alcoholic. I'm sure there are legions of sober ones out there—I just never have managed to find one of 'em. No, I take that back—the guy who painted our lake house porch was an absolutely sober, delightful, and punctual young man. Okay, so there's one.

When I found myself the sole possessor of what had been my first marital home, I decided it needed more improvements than just the reduction of inhabitants to make it livable, and painting was on the list of requirements. I have no recollection of how I came to make the acquaintance of the two individuals I was to hire for this task but I'll certainly never forget THEM. Tom and Ed. Ed was burly and brash—also big. Tom was slight, shy, and sweet—imagine Barney Fife was drinking himself to death and right before he succeeded in that, you hired him to paint your living room—that was Tom.

I came home one day and they had taken my front door off to paint it—red, as it happens—so I was able to just walk right in, with no worries of possibly knocking one of them off a ladder as I opened the door. As it turned out, there was no need to worry about the possibility of knocking either of them off a ladder because they were both sprawled out on my living room floor, dead-ass drunk and sleeping like big ole nasty babies.

Stepping over the beer cans, the bodies, and the abandoned, stiffening paint brushes, I made my way to the solitary sanctuary of my bedroom to place a call for consult and commiseration to my sole steadfast source for these and all things—my sister, Judy. While we were lamenting the sorriness of this state of affairs, it managed to move itself from the bad category over to the upper quadrant of worse when I peeked out of my room to check on the situation and saw that the dead had apparently risen and departed the premises—leaving my living room not only drunk-free, which was a definite improvement, but also DOOR-free, which was maybe not so great. It was to remain in both states for two solid weeks until they finally returned. The only reason I am still alive to relate this story is that it occurred in 1983, probably the last year it was safe enough in that neighborhood to do something as stupid as leave the front door off a house for two minutes, let alone two weeks.

Anyway, all that is to say that my own personal experience with Things Being Painted Red was not sufficiently fun so as to inspire repetition and certainly not enough to broaden the scope to include a whole town, cute shoes notwithstanding.

You will, one day, find that the memory of the days of your shoeful indiscretions will kindle not so much nostalgia as incredulity that you ever sought out, spent good money on, and then actually spent TIME in shoes that today you would think snacking on after they'd stepped in dog-doo would be preferable to having to wear them.

No, when you see some darlin' young thing prance by precariously perched on top of a pair of four-inch Jimmy Choos, you will NOT be envious in the slightest. You will, rather, wince inside on behalf of her poor feet that are, at that very moment, storing up piles of painful memories in their soles with which to torture her just a few years hence.

Often the Big Panty Conversion and the Comfy Shoe Switch coincide but it's not carved in stone. Big Panties are generally discovered during pregnancy and we never willingly give them up for long after that. Usually, the only way we ever give them up is in the case of Divorce and/or Death, which results in a repeat plunge into the dating pool, thereby unfortunately necessitating a resumption of Pretty Underwear for a time, but once we either settle in with a new man or get reeeeeally happy without one, it's amazing how fast we find that "the dryer ate my thongs" and Queen Comfort reigns supreme once more.

Even though the appeal of mile-high strappy sandals mercifully diminishes for us, the lure of a pair of really cool boots seems to be more enduring. First of all, it's possible to find fabulous boots that do not also have ridiculously high heels, and they keep our feet warm in the winter—the importance of which increases for us with time. But equally important, I think, is the fully empowered mind-set that comes with the donning of really cool boots—we're comfy, we're warm—we can handle ANYTHING—and if not, then we can at least kick the crap out of it.

Geezer Power Point

Bwahahahaha! I just saw a mention on the Internet that "Patio Dresses Are ALL the RAGE!" And I was thinking to myself that I couldn't believe that in 2008, any copywriter anywhere is still declaring that something is "all the rage." It just sounds so hokey, doesn't it? HOWEVER, I must admit—I did click on the link provided by those words and guess what popped up on my screen? A MUUMUU! And then, of course, I KNEW what was going on. The designer, the manufacturer, and the copywriter are all really clever OLD PEOPLE—and they have resurrected the MUUMUU, only the best, most comfy garment ever devised—renamed it the "patio dress," and declared it to be ALL the RAGE. Once again, old age and treachery triumph over youth and beauty. Here's TO the Patio Dress—and pass the Chocolate Stuff!

Asset-Preserving Tip

If you ever find yourself mentally mired in what seems to be a non-navigable mess—what you need to do is just take a break from thinking about it all for a while—let your mind focus on something else, something totally unrelated, for a bit—and come back to address the problem later. There are two options here: one is to declare yourself Queen of Whatever, decide that, no matter what, you are COMING to Jackson, Mississippi, the third weekend in March to BE IN the Sweet Potato Queens® Million Queen March with your fellow Queens from around the world—and that being said, it is time to PLAN YOUR OUTFIT! There is NOTHING ON EARTH quite so pleasantly distracting as this planning process—probably only the Parade Itself will surpass.

Your SECOND option would be to put on a pair of tight shoes and walk around in 'em for a couple of hours. You will absolutely forget ALL OTHER problems, I guarantee it.

Both of these will totally work—but, now, reckon which option I'd pick for you, darlin'?

BULLETIN

Just in from U.K.—Big Panties Save House!

Kentucky Queen Cheryl alerted me to this amazing story from northern England, where it seems a woman's home was saved from what could have been a horrific fire—by the timely and fortuitous application to the blaze of a big giant pair of panties. The woman was away from home at the time and her teenage son John and her nephew Darren were frying bread—which is apparently a normal thing to do with bread in England— perhaps they were making French toast? Who knows— deciphering British English can be so tricky at times—anyway, the "extractor fan"—which I took to be the Vent-A-Hood— suddenly fell out and landed on top of the stove and the whole thing burst into flames.

The lights went out and the room quickly filled with smoke. John initially made matters worse by dumping water on the flames. Clearly, John never took seventh-grade home economics with Mrs. Boone at Peeples Junior High School in Jackson, Mississippi, or he would have known better than to do such a bonehead thing. Luckily for John and the house itself, Darren had apparently received proper kitchen-fire procedural instructions from Mrs. Boone's British counterpart because he knew that what was needed was a large something or other with which to SMOTHER the flames. In the dim smokiness, he couldn't really see well enough to locate a lid for the pan and he didn't recall there being any fire blankets lying about; however, he did remember that there was a pile of laundry in the room nearby.

Quickly locating the clothes heap, he blindly snatched what felt to be a sufficiently largish item off the top and, after dousing it with water under the tap, he utilized the wet garment to handily extinguish the inferno. The house/day–saving item was later determined to be an enormous pair of panties—they call them knickers over yonder—belonging to the lady of the saved house.

She arrived home shortly after the crisis had been averted and happily posed for a news photo—holding up her own charred size 20s, grinning from ear to ear. (Personally, I do believe I would rather be burned up in the house fire myownself than have to pose for a picture for the NEWSPAPER holding up my big giant underwear that they PUT OUT THE FIRE WITH for all the world to witness. But I'm sure that's just me—I'm sensitive like that. I don't mind WEARING them—prefer them, actually, as we've already established—but I don't want to SHOW them to anybody.)

But this is just one more prime example of the Benefits of Big Giant Panties. If Darren had blindly snatched and grabbed up a little teeny-tiny thong—the story would have been a tragic one indeed. As it was, the headline read: FIRE FIRE, PUT PANTS ON FRYER!

More Important Panty News

Just this very day, there is an article in the paper about a woman suing the world's foremost perpetrator of pretty but painful panties for something approaching the gross national product, plus 10 percent for mental suffering, because she suffered PERMANENT CORNEAL DAMAGE when a metallic decorative something or other on a THONG flew off and hit her with excessive force smack in the eyeball.

Horrifying story—and made all the more so by the very fact of its total *avoidability*. Those of us clad in big, giant, soft Russian immigrant underwear breathe a sigh of relief that OUR eyeballs are safe from random attack by crazed, embellished, minuscule panties and we are smug in our comfort and safety. OTHER PEOPLE'S eyeballs could be in danger, should they happen to SEE us, accidentally or on purpose, in our big'uns— but clearly, that is THEIR problem and none of our own.

~8~

Who Exactly Calls the Wind "Mariah"?

I grew up listening to the Kingston Trio sing a song that has baffled me from the first time I heard it. It's says "away out here"—without ever making clear just where that might be—"they"—without ever a hint as to who "they" ARE—have a name for rain and for fire and for the wind. It seems that, according to the trio, "they" call the rain "Tess," "they" call fire "Joe," and "they" refer to the wind as "Mariah." Never in the song does it tell who these people are nor does it even try to explain WHY they have assigned human-type names to these elements of nature or how they came to choose those particular names. I've always found this to be a very odd song.

I've never come across anything in American literature to support this musical claim—that there are people out there somewhere on a first-name basis with wind, rain, and fire. If you know of any reference source that might be helpful to my understanding of this—please e-mail me posthaste at hrhjill@ sweetpotatoqueens.com. I cannot wait to hear from you.

It rains here all the time—nobody has ever called it Tess. I know people whose actual houses have burned completely up—there was no talk of Joe. I checked and this is not a Yankee deal—my mama is a Yankee and she doesn't know any Tess, Joe, or Mariah—we can't blame it on them.

Well, anyway, "Mariah" blows through down here quite often at certain times of the year. Once in a while, we will get the afterblow of a pretty big wind—we generally call 'em hurricanes and I can't recall one ever being named Mariah, but we also get our very own smaller but nonetheless powerful versions of these storms and nobody calls THEM anything but "tornado."

And that's what I had in mind to talk about when I started this rant—tornadoes and how they can sometimes reveal some real innerestin' stuff about folks when they least expect it. You can live with or around 'em your whole life and think you know pretty much all there is to know about 'em and then whoosh!— let a tornado rip through the area and you might just be surprised what's under their personal rocks.

First of all, just because somebody's past a "certain age," don't be thinking they're grown UP in any way that might be indicative of anything you could have come to think of as wise, reasonable, and/or mature. You have only to observe their reactions to stressful, fight-or-flight-type situations to get a picture of what I'm talking about.

I know two women—we can call them Tammy 1 and Tammy 2—who, on a good day—one that would include fair weather—both of them are just as rational and smart—they're not brain surgeons but they coulda been if they'd been so inclined—but let a tornado siren go off and all that good sense just blows right out the window on the first stiff breeze.

Tammy 1's severe weather response is to immediately locate and pick up her purse. If she's got her purse strap on her shoulder, she's good to go—or blow away, as the case may be. Now, one qualification on this—if it should happen to be the middle of the night, she will first put on a housecoat and THEN put her purse on her shoulder and consider herself well prepared for any outcome. I guess she imagines that if she is blown into the next county, she will be soooo glad she's not stranded over there naked and without her handbag.

Tammy 2 is not as fearless as Tammy 1—purse or no purse, Tammy 2 is terrified of tornadoes. Well, actually, she's not so much afraid of the tornadoes as she is of the possible result of a tornado hitting on top of wherever she's hiding. She is deathly afraid that one day a tornado will swoop down out of the sky when she least expects it and leave her to be interviewed as a survivor on national TV—with unsupported bosoms. Yes, Tammy 2 has a phobia for which I have been unable to find a medical name: she fears that she will be struck by and survive a tornado—at such a time when she is not wearing a bra and all her lingerie will have been blown to the next county—and that she will then be interviewed on national television with saggy tits. Let's be clear about this now—she does not fear being discovered and displayed while naked and/or dead—just that she will somehow end up on national news—with no bra under her T-shirt.

She seriously worries about this every time there is a storm warning. I think her insurance company should pay for her to have a breast lift just so the poor thing can sleep braless at night without worrying about ending up looking like she belongs in a National Geographic special.

And just when you think you reeeeally have got somebody pegged—along comes ole Mariah blowing their little secrets out in the yard for the whole world to view. Picture it: storm passes and neighbors venture outside to see that only one house has been damaged—the one belonging to the stodgy old couple down the block who happened to be out of town when Mariah came calling. The neighborhood guys took it upon themselves to do what neighbors do in these situations—help out. So they were going all around, retrieving the household goods of Mr. and Mrs. Oldfolks. There was no problem with determining ownership since only the one house was damaged.

Imagine their surprise when after picking up about a hundred pairs of Mrs. Oldfolks's undies, they came to the shocking realization that there was not a single CROTCH in a single pair of any of those panties. The guys were so mortified at discovering Mrs. Oldfolks's spicy little secret that they threw all her underwear away and pretended like they never saw it. They were also pret-ty surprised to discover that Mr. and Mrs. Oldfolks were not wheezer-geezers after all—to the contrary, they apparently had A Lot Going On. Suffice it to say, Mr. Oldfolks was accorded a whole new respect from the guys at neighborhood gatherings from then on.

9

Isn't that just a fabulous Queen name? I do believe that sometimes we need a different name to call the Selves that surface, often unbidden, from within our very own personages, don't we? I'm told that in some cultures, parents name children at birth for qualities they hope they will come to embody, and then at some point in adulthood, the children choose other names for themselves—again, to represent qualities that they themselves hope to grow to embody.

That's a good plan for us all as we consider names for our alter egos, I think. I'll tell you, when I ordered my first treasured pair of genuine Dr. Bukk's Teef (www.drbukk.com), I went right on and joined the Bukk Fambly, choosing for myself a new name by which I could be identified in the Bukk Fambly Tree. It is believed, by the Bukks and by anybody who ever owned a pair of these most fine Teef, that one is so completely transformed by the donning of the Teef, a whole new person is born and thus a new name is required. My Bukk Fambly name is GEMI MOORE. I do try to live up to it every day.

I wrote about Dr. Bukk in my very first book, *The Sweet Potato Queens' Book of Love,* but it's been a long time since I mentioned them to y'all and so if you don't already own a pair of GENUINE Dr. Bukk's—you need to go right this second to www.drbukk.com and git you some, darlin', and by all MEANS, tell 'em I sent you!

There are crummy knockoffs but nothing compares in quality. First of all, Dr. Bukk's are made right over yonder in Georgia and there is NO LEAD in them—which is SUCH a plus. I mean, I love my Teef, but even I am not willing to DIE for them. Second—and just as important, I believe—they fit so well, you can even DRINK while wearing them. Undreamed-of bonus, right there. I love the "Cowcatcher" model—my seester, Judy, has those and I'm wantin' 'em bad for myownself. I have "Summer Teef" (some are here, some are not) and also "Sole Survivor." They have a number of new models that I am coveting as well. Please, when you get yours—send me a photo of yourself! Send 'em to me at hrhjill@sweetpotatoqueens.com. REALLY, I wanna see you in your Teef, so be sure and bring 'em with you when you come to the PARADE in Jackson—we can have a group photo made.

I'm thinking of getting my still underage daughter to get me a few fake IDs for Gemi Moore and some of my Other Personas that pop out from time to time.

And while I'm on the subject—just how is it that there are all these totally believable fake IDs available today? I swear, there is a kid around here putting himself through college selling fake IDs—I think he's got, like, a real official driver's-license-maker thing from Arkansas or somewhere—got it off the Internet. Now, THERE'S something. How is it that you can buy—no, not you, YOUR KID—can buy, right off the Net—no doubt using YOUR credit card, though—something like that that surely is illegal? I mean, don't you figger it's illegal? Otherwise, why do I bother fooling with the Department of Transportation every few years, getting an updated driver's license? Of course, from THEM, I can still have the same weight that I had on there from when I was, like, twenty-two or something. If I tried to do that with this KID, he'd prolly take one look at me and say, yeah, RIGHT, lady. Little asshole. He charges a hundred bucks for 'em, too.

At least he's got a JOB . . . of sorts—more than I can say for MY kid. Of course, she's not risking jail time by lolling around, sponging off me—dismemberment and death, perhaps, on a given day—but certainly not jail time.

Did I Say That?

Queen Janice had come to the Sweet Potato Queens® Million Queen March™ in Jackson, Mississippi, the third beautiful weekend of one particular March and went home a Changed Woman. Upon her return to Nashvegas, she developed a problem with the seatbelt mechanism in her car and, not wishing to risk her very life any longer than absolutely necessary, she betook herself forthwith to the auto repair shop, even though to do so constituted a full-fledged errand . . . and you know how we all feel about those.

Nonetheless, the bullet was bitten and her turn with the mechanic came sooner than expected and she explained to him her problem. He listened gravely to her and then solemnly examined the mechanism, paying special attention to the buckle. Gazing thoughtfully into it, he remarked that there was "something in it," and with that he commenced to fishing around inside it with his screwdriver, and what should he pull out but a single black feather.

Without a word, he looked at the feather and then at her, and then back at the feather. He then resumed his screwdriver fishing expedition, which yielded quite a few more bird hairs. Now, Queen J admits to being over fifty and possibly JUST a tad overserved at the dinner table, although I am certain she is exaggerating that part. Her hair is gray because she refuses to dye it and end up looking "like I'm wearing a bad Elvis wig—

like some folks I know"—but politely does not name, naturally. She can tell that the mechanic is not totally comfortable asking her the question that he feels, nonetheless, that he MUST ask her: "Ma'am, have you been wearing a feather boa while driving this car?"

And you know how it is, your Inner Queen just WILL pop out sometimes when you least expect her to, and so it was not "Janice" but Queen JaJa GaBoa who gave him a sidelong glance from underneath her thick black eyelashes (all natural, of course) and said, in a Southern accent so thick it would scarcely roll off her tongue, "Why-y-y-y . . . ye-e-e-es . . . I ha-a-ve!"

Totally bowled over by the right-before-his-very-eyes transformation of his formerly normal customer, he gaped at her for a long moment as if he expected her to break out into a Fan Dance next. He finally pulled himself out of his trance, went back to fishing feathers, and stammered, "Well, I-I-I've ab-b-bout g-g-got it f-fixed here, j-j-just try not to w-w-wear it while you're d-d-drivin' next time, ma'am, okay?!" She huskily assured him that she "wouldn't DRE-E-AM of it and thank you SO much for ALL your he-e-lp."

She had a fair-sized chuckle to herself as she drove away, secure in the knowledge that she'll be getting much improved service THERE in the future.

Not Particularly Queenly, but Certainly Sna

I love those little short stories that come out in the newspap
just a paragraph and a half usually—they come from a wire
vice and fill in gaps, I suppose. They're nearly always way m
intriguing than the stuff they've devoted whole FEET of colun
space to—and it's always just enough to make me wonder wh;
the hell was REALLY going on there.

FOR INSTANCE: Last year, there was this teeny-tiny mention in our local paper of an event in a small town in Pennsylva-
nia. It seemed that—for some undisclosed reason—the police
had been summoned to a private residence—by person or persons unknown—and once on the scene, the woman, with whom
I assume the authorities had been summoned to deal, met the
officers at the door and "held them at bay" (I love that term) by
"brandishing" POISONOUS SNAKES at them.

There was no information at ALL about what exactly it was
that she had been doing to spur the unknown party(ies) to call
the Law on her—no explanation of how come her to have all
those poisonous snakes—didn't even tell us how many or what
kind, eggzackly—nor what might have led to her snatch up a
coupla handfuls of 'em on her way to answer the front door—
was she always toting them around by the fistful or was this a
special circumstance? They didn't even describe the alleged
"brandishing" so we don't know if she was waving them around
in big circles or waggling them, in a taunting fashion, right up

165

close under the cops' noses or WHAT exactly? NONE of that was explained and I'm quite certain I am not the only person in the country who read that little blurb and wondered to herself, *What the fuck?*

But her response when asked for a statement before her sentencing (they didn't even tell what all she was charged with and convicted of)—to house arrest and probation—was one of my All-Time Favorite Snappy Comebacks to a Stupid Question—this ranks right up there with "That's My Story and I'm Sticking to It." What she offered by way of, I suppose, explanation and/or justification for her now-admitted acts that included, but I guess were not limited to, Willful Poisonous Snake Brandishment at a Law Enforcement Officer was this—and only this: "I JUST WASN'T IN THE RIGHT FRAME OF MIND THAT NIGHT."

Now, THERE is a By-God ANSWER, I'm sayin'! I am so lovin' this woman! I just want to sit down with her and have her tell me the Whole Story—I especially want to know ALL about her frame of mind that night—what the "right" frame would have been and what all led up to her being in the "wrong" frame and, of course, who was responsible for THAT and where is he now— did she feed him to the snakes, I hope? I fear this will be one of those things in life that I just never get the chance to do and it will haunt me. When I am a thousand years old, sitting in the nursing home in my diaper and staring out at nothing, looking blank, if you ask me what I'm thinking about—this could very well be it.

But Even at Our Worst,
We Make More Sense Than "Some"

Some of my Queens have shared with me that they often suffer great torment regarding their Queenly Transformation at the hands of their most loved ones—namely, their wretched teenagers and/or their own personal husbands, who ought to know better.

Regarding the wretched teenagers—or even now-grown children who certainly were ONCE wretched teenagers—who dare to express shock, horror, and dismay, accompanied by a fair dose of humiliation and embarrassment, at the thought and/or sight of you, their mom, engaging in full cavort-mode while wearing all manner of sparkly, glittery, spangly, and feathery garb and also demonstrating your unswerving intent to carry on with this outlandish display IN PUBLIC—yeah, regarding them—BWAHAHAHAHA! SERVES 'EM RIGHT, doesn't it? Is it not one of the Fondest Dreams of Any Parent of a Teenager that they will be blessed to just live long enough to one day BE an embarrassment to that teenager? (THE Fondest Dream is, of course, to be blessed to live long enough to see that kid with his or her OWN teenager—but Causing Them Embarrassment is one of the top Dreams, for sure.)

So, I'd say, unless you've got them shrieking "OH MY GOD!" and running to lock themselves in their rooms—you're not wearing QUITE ENOUGH bling. Just keep adding rhinestones until you get the desired reaction, then you'll know your outfit is perfect.

As to the HUSBANDS who dare to not only LOOK askance at your Royal Garments but further compound their error by VOICING some unsolicited and unwelcome opinion regarding the supposed "suitableness" of such attire and behavior, let us consider for a moment some of HIS OWN pursuits and weigh THEM on this same scale.

For your consideration: You are being questioned and/or criticized by an individual who will crawl out of your very own warm bed and get up in the absolute DARK of night to dress up like a TREE, and he can't tolerate your cologne but he will douse himself with a foul elixir with an equally foul name, like "Doe in Heat," and go hide in the woods, just on the off chance that a boy deer will happen by and he can shoot at it. Sometimes he wears bobcat urine—no one knows why.

Now, I ask you—do you REALLY CARE about this person's opinion of your outfit and Queenly Intentions? Good, glad we got that settled.

He Did Know the Job was Dangerous When He Took It

Once upon a time, not so very long ago, there was a husband of a Queen who insisted on coming along with his Queenly Wife and her Queenly Girlfriends to Jackson, Mississippi, for the Sweet Potato Queens® Million Queen March™ weekend. He willingly agreed to all the terms they specified for his attendance to be approved—those being for the most part that he would be around to tote, fetch, and pay for things and assert loudly and repeatedly to everyone within human earshot that THEY themselves were, in fact, not only the Cutest Things in the Whole Town, They Were Furthermore the Cutest Things He Had Ever Seen Anywhere at Any Time in His Whole EN-tire Life, but other than that, he understood that he was to be Wallpaper.

Whatever They Said, he assured them in his fevered desperation to tag along, and they finally assented and allowed him to accompany them. There were constant reminders of His Word during the long car trip to Jackson and one final unified chorus as they all exited their vehicle upon arrival at the Jackson Hilton. Yes, yes, he understood and he would not be ANY trouble, he promised.

So, of course, what did he do but come down with APPENDICITIS that very night, just LIKE a man, I swear. Lucky for him, he was in the company of a pack of nurses who identified his symptoms quickly enough that it did not disrupt their evening much at all. They did take time out to PERSONALLY drive him TO the hospital on their way to the SPQ™ Ball, in their full regalia—although there were perfectly good ambulances nearby that could have spared them the time and trouble—nurses AND SAINTS is all they are, obviously.

He was maybe a leetle bit surprised, I think, when they LEFT him at the emergency room, but they reminded him—a deal's a deal—made sure the nurses on duty promised to keep the pain meds coming—gave him a little pat and told him they WOULD come back and fetch him for the drive home—he did not need to worry about getting a cab to the Hilton or anything. They're coming to take you to the OR any minute now, you just sit tight after surgery, take your drugs, watch huntin' on the teevee in your room and we'll be by to get you on Sunday afternoon—BYE-BYE!

As it turned out, he was released from the hospital late Saturday afternoon—after the parade but before Pearls & PJ's—which was SO lucky for THEM because that meant he was available to go down to the Hilton lobby to fetch their coffee on Sunday morning before they went to the Bathrobe Brunch™. He was thrilled that he was at least able to provide this small service for them. He still wants to come back next year. Now, that's a Good Man, right there—a true Spud Stud™—and we LOVE him for it!

~10~

Dear God, Please Send Children

At nearly every wedding I've attended in recent years, I've been struck by a recurring theme in the prayers. Somewhere in one of the prayers in all of these different ceremonies, there has been a humble entreaty that the Almighty bless this union with children. At the most recent wedding we attended, the plea was issued at the rehearsal dinner, during the wedding, and again at the reception—and the ante was upped in that MANY children were requested. I was nonplussed.

But then, I was having a before-church conversation with my good friend "G." Having just returned from visiting his finally-grown-up-and-happily-married son, he was beaming and going on at some length about the rapturous joys of Grandparenting that can come to one when one has survived the childhood and often overlong adolescence of one's own children.

He waxed hysterically sentimental about the charmed and charming teen years of his precious daughter, "N," compared to the way, way overlong adolescence of his way wayward son, "T." Truth be told, son T liked to have driven G plumb over the edge many times—many, MANY times. If we want to be completely honest about the whole thing, G got to looking with great longing at that edge before T met and fell way off into love with a darlin' girl, and that little girl got hold of T and inspired him to grow the hell up.

In the years before her arrival, G quite often received those dreaded middle-of-the-night phone calls that NEVER bode well for anybody concerned. He would frantically fumble for the phone and try to focus his eyes on the clock and his mind on the call, eke out some groggy semblance of a "Hello," only to be greeted on the other end by an inappropriately chipper T who hailed his dad with a hearty "HEY, DAD! HOW YA DOIN'?!"

To which G would logically respond, "T, it's two-thirty in the MORNING. Why are you calling me—what is wrong— what have you done?" T would answer with a happy, oh-gosh-darn tone, "Well, Dad, I'm in Tupelo and I was in this bar . . ." (It should be noted that T nearly always went at least three hours away from home to commit these infractions, making it even more unhandy to go and extricate him from whatever circumstances he had gotten himself mired in. In this case, he was a good four hours away. The calls ALWAYS involved "a bar" somewhere, naturally.)

So, T says, he was in this bar and he got in a fight. "Are you in jail?" G naturally asked. "Well, no, Dad, I'm not in jail but I am bleeding and I was just wondering what you thought I ought to do?" "T, just go to the emergency room and see if you need stitches—do you think you need stitches, son?" "Well, I might, Dad, it's kinda SQUIRTIN' OUT everywhere—what do you think I ought to do?" "T—GO TO THE EMERGENCY ROOM, NOW!" G hangs up the phone and lies there in the dark, staring blindly, wondering if there is any possibility of sleep returning to him this night, and the phone rings again. "HEY, DAD! Say, are you coming to take me to the emergency room?" "T—I'm FOUR HOURS away—YOU ARE IN TUPELO—YOU'LL BLEED TO DEATH IF YOU WAIT FOR ME TO COME UP THERE—just hold a towel over whatever it is that's bleeding . . ." "It's the top of my ear, Dad." "Hold a towel over your EAR and GO to the emergency room, T. Do NOT call me back until you have done that." "Uh, okay, Dad."

And then it all became crystal clear to me—the reason for the kid prayers at the weddings—(which, clearly, vengeful parents are slipping into the service)—and the reason for G's sparkling disposition that Sunday morning after his visit with T and his wife. T's wife had just presented them all with a brand-new

BABY BOY and G is now praying to be around for at least another eighteen years.

Grandkids are the definite upside of Geezerdom. They are precious beyond words when they're little—and it brings to mind the good old days when your own kids were babies—and then, when they turn into Teenage Mutant Hounds from Hell—you can just laugh and laugh from the soothing sanctuary of your own home, far, far away. Vengeance may indeed be His, according to the Lord, but ain't it swell when He shares just a little bit of it?

~11~

Travel

Travel has certainly changed a good bit for me over the course of my life. As a child, terrified of nearly everything in the Universe with the one remotely possible exception of my own shadow (maybe, I don't really remember—coulda been scared of that, too—prolly was), I never went anywhere—ANYWHERE—without one—but preferably both—of my parents.

In the summers of my twelfth and thirteenth years, my best friend, Rhonda, and I would go on business trips with my daddy, who was in the insurance industry. He would need to meet with his agents in various and sundry little towns all over Mississippi, Louisiana, and Arkansas, and Rhonda and I thought it was just THE best thing in the world to ride along with him—for hours upon hours on highways, byways, and narrow, rutted two-lane roads—stopping at many roadside mom-and-pop stores—and every single Stuckey's—along the way to restock on sugar and stupid souvenirs, both of which we could never get enough of.

I remember the first time I became aware of the existence of Stuckey's. Can't tell you where we were traveling to or from but I can tell you that somewhere along our route, I suddenly saw, outside my backseat window, a sign proclaiming that it was only 153 miles to STUCKEY'S. In just a minute, there was another sign advising me that we had moved one mile closer to STUCKEY'S—and so it went for the subsequent 143 miles. There was a small roadside sign at every single mile, feeding my frenzy for whatever this mystical thing called "Stuckey's" was. On these signs, there were no words or graphics offering me so much as a hint concerning the nature of this too-slowly-approaching wonder—"144 miles to Stuckey's" was all I got until "143" came up. It was like "99 Bottles of Beer on the Wall," only slower and not to music.

I couldn't imagine what could be so all-fired important about this thing called Stuckey's as to require so very much consistent advance notice, but I knew that, whatever it was, I did NOT want to miss it.

At about ten miles out, Stuckey's increased the pressure by erecting huge billboards with mentions of what all I would find in plentiful supply when I finally arrived at Stuckey's. Each mile we traveled brought me that much closer to "PECAN LOGS!" and "DIVINITY!" "CLEAN RESTROOMS" at least got some response out of Mama, who declared that she would believe THAT when she saw it with her own two eyes.

She's a Potty Animal

A clean public restroom was the Holy Grail for Mama, and it was just about as elusive, as far as I can recollect. I can't actually recall her ever, even once, walking into one and breathing a big sigh of relief, delight, or satisfaction at what met her gaze. My memory banks are overflowing with her most common reactions, which included but were not limited to horrified breathing—on both the inhale and the exhale—which gave you a shocked, fainty kind of gasp on the front end and a sharp, disgusted puff on the finish—accompanied by eyes that were at first bugged out as wide as possible with eyebrows yanked up around her hairline, followed by the squintiest possible squint, eyebrows lowered and drawn together tight in the middle of her much-furrowed forehead. Due to the horror of the sight before her, words would often escape her momentarily, but when she did find a few, the first couple were most likely to be "MERCIFUL HEAVENS!" (Never once in my EN-tire life have I ever heard my mama express shock or dismay with a resounding and well-earned "HOLY SHIT!" which, as you oughta know by NOW, is one of my most oft-used epithets. I can't recall right off where I learned it, but I can tell you for sure, it was most assuredly NOT from Mama.)

At any rate, my seester, Judy, and I would hear that "MERCIFUL HEAVENS!" as Mama led the way into the privy and we would know pretty much what we could expect to see when we rounded the corner. Mama always went in first, to survey the territory and devise a plan. A plan was needed to ensure that we somehow managed to relieve ourselves in the blighted facilities available without actually touching ANY surface in the area with ANY part of our anatomies. We could not touch the doors, the walls, or the receptacle that held the toilet paper—only the paper itsveryself.

But first, Mama would go into the stall and cover every visible surface with miles and piles of toilet paper. I wonder how many acres of timberlands were deforested because of her papering proclivities. Often, by the time her work was complete, we could not even see the water in the toilet bowl. Once the entire toilet and surrounding area were completely swathed in its protective toilet paper armor—then and only then would one of us be allowed to enter the stall and assume the rigorous posture of the Female Attempting the Torturous and Very Delicate Process of Endeavoring to Urinate While Standing. (I am certain this must be one of THE most advanced yoga postures of all. I bet there are ancient Sanskrit scrolls with drawings depicting it as one of the last postures to be mastered before transcending this world entirely.)

But we were expected to master it and assume it WHEN-EVER we used any restroom that was not in our own personal home or that of someone we were either related to or knew so well we were practically related to them. I mean, if we weren't allowed to touch the DOOR HANDLE of the stall—lest we contract some hideous, painful, disfiguring, deadly, and, of course, socially embarrassing disease—do you imagine for one second that we were allowed to have the slightest whisper of a brush with the true epicenter of worldwide nasty germiness—the actual COMMODE itself?

I can't really fathom what Mama would have done if this had ever happened—either by accident or design—the thought of defying Mama's Restroom Edicts never occurred to us, and our youthful THIGHS never failed us—quiver though they might, they always held our Precious Private Parts well in the clear of those beshrouded bowls. Faced with failure, I suppose she would have had no choice but to have us shot on the spot—as the only humane solution. "John, hunny, bring the pistol—the girls sat on this nasty pot, you're gon' have to put 'em down!"

The touching taboo, of course, also extended to the flushing handle of the toilet. No matter how high above the floor it might be situated, we were commanded and expected to reach it and somehow push it down with our foot. This feat alone explains the amazing high-kick prowess of Southern dance troupes and cheerleaders. We—all of us—have been working on that move since we were potty-trained. Don't think for one second that this stringent bathroom ritual was peculiar to just my own Yankee mama. No, indeed—it's ALL of 'em. Certainly no female born and reared by a mama who was born and reared south of the Mason-Dixon has EVER sat down on a public toilet OR flushed one with anything but her foot.

If you accidentally dropped something—ANYTHING—Hope diamond, the actual tablets containing the Ten Commandments, your little brother, what-EV-ER—it was gone—into the trash it went—and no amount of tearful pleading could spare it from the waste bin—IN it MUST go—BUT NOT WITH YOUR BARE HANDS!

If Mama happened to be preoccupied with her own THIGH-throbbing, hiney-hovering peeing performance and was therefore unavailable for personally handling the disposal of the floor-sullied article, she would holler instructions to you on the proper method to be employed. As if she could see you reaching bare-handed toward it, she would bark an echoing preemptive "DON'T TOUCH IT!" from inside the stall. No, you must first roll off approximately 2.75 miles of toilet paper (she could tell from the repetitive sound as you spun the roll of paper when you had amassed a sufficient quantity to make an effective germ barrier) and ball it up, over, and around the now-ruined-beyond-reclaim item on the floor and then pick up the entire mass, with your hand extended as far out in front of you as physically possible, and carry it over to the garbage pail, the swinging door of which you must also somehow NOT touch with your naked hand as you make your deposit. Your high kick would get yet another workout and you would have achieved an aerobic state from the absolutely futile sobbing you'd been doing ever since your Prized Possession first slipped from your grasp and landed with a telltale whump, thump, jingle, or swish on the floor. Whatever the sound—Mama heard it and knew in an instant what it represented—and you knew it, too—whatever it was—it was a Major Loss to YOU. And not only would Mama not relent on her iron-clad rule in this regard but there was also a very high probability that there would be further personal consequences for you as well on account of didn't she just finish telling you to leave that in the car? And rest assured, whatever it was, you were NOT getting another one—EVER—and maybe NEXT time you'd MIND her.

As I think on this, I see that there could be substantial savings available to any and all persons and businesses in the South that provide public restrooms for women—savings in water, cleaning supplies, and labor utilized in the sanitizing of those facilities. There is really no point to cleaning them because nobody's ever going to come in contact with anything in there anyway. Just make sure you've got about eight gajillion rolls of toilet paper in stock at all times.

Dubious Championship
Brings Out Yankee-Style Snark

One restroom stands out in the deepest recesses of my childhood memories as the #1 Nastiest Place on the Planet. Since attaining adulthood, I have traveled the world a goodly bit and I have seen some Nasty—but no matter what, no matter where, there is one place that has not and will not, in my opinion, ever be surpassed for its utter, complete, and constant state of indescribable filth. It was the ladies' restroom in the Texaco station in Kosciusko, Mississippi, and desperation dictated its use on occasion when we passed through there on the way out to my grandparents' house in Ethel—which, as you know, is a suburb of Kosciusko. Urgent calls of nature drove me to it many times in the years from about 1956 until around 1965, and I don't think it was ever cleaned before or during that time. Furthermore, I think that before we could enter it, they had to run out the dozen or so wild hogs that apparently dwelled within, if one could believe what all one's senses were telling one.

Not only did it never fail to rate a "MERCIFUL HEAVENS" from her, that restroom actually could and did bring out the Yankee in my mama. As I said before—my own personal mama is a Yankee. Well, she could be and probably is. She was adopted, and no matter where she may have actually come into this world, she grew up in Grosse Pointe, Michigan, and thus, no matter how long she lives in Mississippi, there are just some Yankeeisms that WILL come out now and again.

The one to which I am referring now is the way she would talk when she wanted to say something snarky to SOME-body but not necessarily EVERY-body in the room. Now, in this situation, Southern women will sort of drop their heads down and to the side and put their hand up sort of in front of their mouths and then say whatever awful thing it is they want to say in that most piercing whisper peculiar to them while they raise their eyebrows and roll their eyes in the general direction of whomever it is that they are talking about who's not supposed to hear them. Mama, on the other hand, being the product if not the offspring of the meanest little German-Yankee woman who ever drew breath, would talk out of one side of her mouth—while not moving the other side—at all. She could—and still can—turn her head just ever so slightly off center so that the side facing the victim shows her lips to be motionless and silent while the side facing the one she was snarking to would have a mouth moving and spewing venom in an only slightly lowered and somewhat guttural tone. It's like half a German ventriloquist.

For example, let's just say a woman walked in whom nobody'd seen in a spell and she had maybe put on a pound or thirty in the interim and she was perhaps moving in a slightly less-than-graceful manner, due, in part, to that additional

weight, and possibly her hair, and makeup were not looking especially fine that day either—well, her Southern "friends" might
be observed thusly: adopting the head and hand posture earlier
described and saying in the aforementioned knifelike inhaled
whisper, "AHHHH, would you look at HER . . . bless her heart!"
But Mama—and her German-Yankee mother before her—
would do that quarter-turn with their heads and out of one side
of their mouths they would utter one word: "Hunyuk."

Now, do not ask me what language that is or what the actual translation of it might be—but to hear one of those women
say it out of the side of her mouth was enough to make me
NEVER want to BE IT, whatever it is. If you've heard the word
before and know anything about it—PLEASE e-mail me at
hrhjill@sweetpotatoqueens.com and 'splain it to me!

Anyway, that nasty restroom would make Mama talk out of
the side of her mouth every time. How in the world did I end up
here? I was talking about me and Rhonda traveling with Daddy
in the summer and then I got off on Stuckey's—oh, yeah, and
that got me off on Mama and her quest for a clean public restroom.

I'll never forget when Mama and I went to Japan and Taiwan.
Suffice it to say, Mama not only failed to find a clean public toilet
over there—she failed to find a TOILET in most places. Them
folks favor the ole hole in the ground over your porcelain throne.
Talk about your excellent THIGH workout—after a month over

there, I swear I could squat two hundred pounds! And if and when perchance you should happen upon an actual terlet, you will find that most of the natives prefer to STAND on the seat. I don't know why that undid Mama so—since she was only gonna cover the entire thing with toilet paper and hover over it anyway, what difference did it make?—nonetheless, she did get evermore wound up over it, let me tell you. But I continue to digress—big surprise—let us return to the Tale of Stuckey's.

But first, could I just say a brief word about Porta Potties and how I would just about rather PIMP (isn't it great that, thanks to text messaging on our cell phones, we now have an actual acronym for "peeing in my pants"—so much to thank technology for) than have to utilize one—preferring the storm to this particular port, but that's just me. Anyway, Queen Lynne told me that she and her friend Queen Jules had attended some major fund-raising event—part indoor, part outdoor—for which they had regrettably worn cute outfits and complementary cute shoes as well, so it was that they found themselves fairly well impaled on those old dilemma horns—having to choose between walking, in their cute and correspondingly UN-comfy shoes, ALL that way back to the main building in order to stand in the lines for the inside cool and clean restrooms OR taking the few steps over to stand in the lines for the outside un-air-conditioned, far-from-sanitary portables. Tortured tootsies yelled the loudest and so the short hop to the hot-and-nasty won.

There were two lines—one for the units marked "Ladies" and the other for those labeled "Either." Now, for me, that begs the question—either or WHAT, exactly? Could be ladies or gentlemen—could be ladies or skanky-ass hos, though. At any rate, there were men and women (of varying demeanor) in the Either line, and they made, I think, the wise choice with that line on account of it just does not take guys very long to pee under any circumstances but the performance time for women is generally substantially increased by the fact that we are hampered by the close quarters and the fact that the stifling heat causes all our clothes to immediately become shrink-wrapped to our bodies, and our horror at our surroundings does little to expedite matters. So at least the men in the Either line offer some hope for a speedier queue.

Sure enough, their gamble paid off and Queens Lynne and Jules quickly found themselves entering the two side-by-side Eithers. Lynne emerged from her sweatbox first and stood waiting and panting in the shade of Jules's Either cubicle until presently, the door swung open and out came the sweaty but strangely ebullient Jules, exclaiming loudly that THAT was, by far and away, the NICEST Porta Potti she had ever had the pleasure of being forced by her throbbing feet to use after ten-thousand other people in the blazing sun.

And what, Queen Lynne wondered aloud, could possibly rate such an effusion of enthusiasm regarding a sweltering, festering public loo? Well, gushed Jules, at least it had that handy little place to put my purse—it must have been designed by a woman; who else would realize how important it is to have a place to put your purse while you pee?

Upon hearing this revelation, Queen Lynne spontaneously erupted with a true belly-grabbing, rolling-on-the-ground "bwahahahaha" that drew quite a curious crowd from the surrounding area. Jules, reigning Queen of Igmos, had, of course, placed her precious Prada purse—smack IN the URINAL of the Either potty. For years now, everyone (with the notable exception of Jules) has so enjoyed that story. Sorry to propagate it, Jules, but—well, naahh, not really—it's too good NOT to. Surely, you're over it by now? No? Oh, well.

Okay—Now, I Swear—Back to Stuckey's . . . Saw It, Had to Have It, Pitched a Fit, Got It—and It's Never Enough

When the Stuckey's signs finally advised me that, in addition to an insulin coma and a nice potty, I could also avail myself of "SOUVENIRS!"—well, I was just about wild to get there.

Fortunately for my parents' fragile sanity, it was not necessary for me to ask that age-old question that reverberates endlessly within the confines of all moving automobiles containing children—and has since moving vehicles were invented—that being, "HOW MANY MORE MILES IS IT?" There was no need to verbalize that query since Mr. Stuckey himself was providing me with a mile-by-mile update on that situation. That service alone should have been enough to endear him to adult motorists everywhere—at least those whose children were old enough to read mile markers.

My burning desire for sweets and souvenirs would not have been enough to persuade Daddy to veer off the path with much frequency—but Stuckey's billboards promised "Clean Restrooms," and that positively guaranteed that I was gonna get to stop at every single one of 'em as long as Mama was in the car. One sampling told me I was not going to become a lifelong fan of the Pecan Logs or the Divinity—but the Souvenirs were quite another matter.

Many of y'all know of my fascination and fondness for all things Tacky, and it is a rare thing indeed to find so MANY genuinely tacky items handily assembled for one in such a convenient location, and then to find that location replicated over and over, every couple of hundred miles or so, is just beyond even the wildest dreams of Tacky Heaven. In one visit to one single Stuckey's, you could buy—or at least lust after—a small wooden outhouse, complete with a patron inside who would turn around, look surprised, and pee on you when you opened the door; a ceramic ashtray shaped like a tiny toilet; a wooden paddle emblazoned with an amusing limerick sure to tickle the funny bone of even the dourest child-beating customer (what a sick slant THAT was on the whole "souvenir" concept): just about anything you can think of covered in tiny seashells (I still have a seashell-covered poodle that is rendered even more lovely by the shade of lavender it is painted); a can of "peanuts" that, when opened, would allow a giant snake made of springs covered in snake-print fabric to fly directly into one's terrified face and would, upon further examination, be found to contain not even one single peanut, thereby compounding an already injurious situation with further insult; anything and everything from salt-and-pepper sets to ball caps depicting either The Lord's Supper, a magnolia, and/or the outline of the state of Mississippi; and all manner of toothpick dispensers—both the passive kind that just sit there holding a wad of toothpicks as well as the active variety that somehow mechanically deliver a single pick into your waiting hand, which would allow one to begin picking one's teeth at the earliest possible moment.

Nabs and Geedunks

On our summer trips with Daddy, though, Mama didn't go along—it was just me and Rhonda and Daddy, and that was some slow-going, let me tell you. Rhon and I wanted to stop at EVERY Stuckey's—in case this one had a larger stock of papier-mâché clowns and genuine birthstone rings—but we didn't like the nabs there, so other stops had to be made with what Daddy considered to be alarming frequency.

Okay, "nabs." Once upon a time, Nabisco sold packs of peanut butter crackers and they were called Nabs. Nowadays, in the South—any pack of snack crackers is called nabs, and we all know what it means, but Outsiders mostly don't. Okay, fine.

When Yankee-boy Jeffrey Gross first met red-dirt Mississippi-boy Allen Payne, a discussion of lunch came up, during the course of which Allen allowed as how he was not in any big hurry to eat just then, having recently had "nabs," and it was weeks before Jeffrey could bring himself to inquire as to what exactly a nab was and how come it to kill one's appetite so completely. He was pretty relieved to learn that the truth was something edible and not contagious.

Anyway, me and my seester, Judy, don't actually care for snack crackers, nabs or otherwise, much at ALL, but we do like the name nabs, so we started calling ALL snacks and party food by that name. Actually, we call just about all food nabs. If we talk on the phone and I tell her I'm going to a gathering at Tammy's house, the first thing Judy will ask is, "Will there be nabs?" Meaning, will there be food? When we used to travel together and we wanted to know where a good restaurant might be found, we would ask everybody we encountered, *"Donde estan nabs?"*—which was particularly confusing to them if we didn't happen to be in, say, Cozumel or some other Hispanic locale— but even if they did speak Spanish, the nabs part would throw 'em. We got a lotta laughs out of it ourownselves, though, and that's all we really care about. Clearly, we have not had ANY trouble finding the nabs, wherever we happen to find ourselves.

So anyway, me and Rhon were not partial to the nabs available at Stuckey's back then—it was all Pecan Logs!—and Divinity! It seemed to us there was only one production run of those products ever in the history of the world and we were pretty sure it was about the same time they made that one Claxton Fruit Cake. We wanted Sugar Babies and Milk Duds and Zero bars and Peanut Butter Logs and Chick-a-Sticks and Fritos and Co-Colas—and occasionally a MoonPie and a Big Orange drink.

Once in a while we would see an establishment that offered soft-serve ice cream—for some unknown reason, Daddy called it a "geedunk." Now, that was Daddy's weakness because it reminded him of homemade ice cream, so no matter how many stops he had already made along the way to appease us, if a geedunk sign appeared on the horizon, he would be whipping in and ordering three. (Two of 'em were for us.)

Daddy never outgrew his lifelong love affair with homemade ice cream and geedunks. It grew at least partially out of his love and admiration for—as well as his competition with—his favorite older sister, Moggie. The "skill" that Moggie possessed—that eluded Daddy his whole entire life—was her ability to stuff about a cup of homemade ice cream into her mouth at one time and then devour it WITHOUT getting that most painful of childhood maladies—BRAIN FREEZE. Daddy watched in worshipful awe his entire life as Moggie would, with a cavalier, devil-may-care look in her eye, load up Maw's biggest cooking spoon with a veritable mountain of homemade ice cream—arguably one of the coldest things on the planet—and stick the whole thing in her mouth and swallow it down without so much as a flinch or a wince, while a mere heaping tablespoonful of the glacial goo would send most mortals, Daddy included, into rigors of head-clasping, facial-contorting, high-pitched-wailing, teeth-grinding, often even ground-rolling frozen-brain misery that seemed to last for hours with no relief.

One childhood brain-freeze experience is USUALLY enough for most humans—that's one lesson we do not EVER want to repeat, and even the most stubborn and slowest-learning amongst us usually spend the rest of our lives giving extremely cold food and beverages the respect they deserve, consuming them with constant caution and care, lest they once again cause us to feel that we have somehow slammed our heads in the car door. A-a-a-a-and then, there was Daddy. He never lost his admiration and envy of Moggie's strange ability—and he could never qui-i-i-ite give up his quest. There was always at least one geedunk each summer that would lure him into just one more attempt at that somewhat dubious unreachable star. He would look at that geedunk and sense Moggie grinning at him, daring him, taunting him to go on—give it a try, little brother—even after she was long-since dead and buried, and her inexplicable gift with her. His recovery time usually allowed me and Rhon to eat a couple more geedunks and re-plenish our stock of *Archie* comic books, so his temerity served us well and we were loath to admonish him for it.

Check-in Chicken Run/Chicken Egg

Sooner or later, no matter how many Stuckey's stops were made, regardless of numerous detours dictated by nabs and geedunks, we would eventually reach our destination—the Holiday Inn of Holly Springs or wherever Daddy's work required him to ap-pear. In those days, in our minds, a Holiday Inn was Lady Lux-ury's very lap—the towels alone were a wonder worth the trip—what with "HOLIDAY INN" actually woven RIGHT INTO the middle of the towel in bright green threads, it was easy to see why it was the national pastime to steal them—and we could not wait to languish in that luxurious lap, especially after a rigorous day of riding in the car and eating crap while reading comic books.

Back then, even mo-tels had bellboys, and no guest was ever allowed to actually sully his hands or strain his back by tot-ing his own luggage through the lobby, across the courtyard, and up the stairs to his second-floor poolside piece of heaven. Daddy did love to torment him some bellboys, too.

There must have been a pretty high turnover rate in the bellboy ranks back then because I never saw one fail to fall for whatever prank Daddy was pulling on him—and so they all had to be new guys. I'm quite certain that NONE of them ever forgot him.

Cases in Point

The bellboys would always precede the guest to the room, unlock and open the door, and then step aside, saying, "Will this be all right?" with an expansive wave of his hand, with an air of "VOILÀ!"—as if revealing to the guest for the first time an opulent suite in the Palace of Versailles. (I never wondered at the time what his response would or could have been should the accommodations ever be found by the guest to be wanting—since every single one of the rooms was 100 percent exactly alike.) One of Daddy's most favoritest things to do involved this little room-approval ritual. Rhon and I could tell right off when he was gonna do it because he would be lagging a bit behind on the trek to the room—we knew this was to allow him room to make his running start—which was in and of itself one of the funniest things I've ever seen in my whole life.

Daddy seldom ran, but when he did it was memorable for two reasons, the first being that he ran like a chicken. If you've never been lucky enough to actually witness a chicken running yourownself, I'll tell you, it's pretty entertaining. Their legs go like lightning but the rest of their bodies are completely motionless. So if you were to film a chicken running—you could divide the screen and the bottom half would show two chicken legs moving back and forth so fast you could hardly see them and the top half would show a chicken just sitting there. If you filmed Daddy running, you would see the same thing. Little skinny legs justa pumpin', and above them, a fairly rotund body at rest. Hilarious to watch. (It should be noted that neither my seester, Judy, nor myself was blessed at birth with the THIGHS of our father—who had lithe and lovely bird legs until the day he died. We both got our mama's THIGHS, and if you were to take a photo of the three of us standing together in swimsuits— well, for starters, you'd need a wide-angle lens, not to mention a stun gun, to capture the vision, since we wouldn't be volunteering to pose for this—it would look like three regular-sized women perched on top of six manatees.)

The second thing you couldn't help but notice about Daddy's chicken run was that it was REEEALLY fast.

So when he was not right on the heels of the bellboy, we knew he was giving himself room for a chicken run at the room. The bellboy would throw open the door for the big reveal, and when Daddy didn't immediately issue an affirmative response to the sight of the room, the bellboy would glance back to see what was going on.

What he would then see was a large fat man chicken-running down the elevated walkway, bearing down on him and the room. Before the bellboy could have any sort of reaction to

THAT sight, Daddy would blur past him into the room, and commence jumping wildly, up and down, to and fro, on all the beds and furniture. After about forty-five seconds of this performance, he would abruptly stop, not even winded, walk over to the bellboy, take the key from his hand, replacing it with a generous tip and ignoring the bug-eyed, slack-jawed expression on his face, and say, "This'll do fine, thankee," and close the door.

Understandably, I think, Rhonda and I never grew tired of this performance nor did any of our friends ever tire of hearing about it. Indeed, not too long ago, I had an e-mail from our old friend Paul Canzoneri asking me did I remember when my daddy used to jump on motel room beds—and it was well over forty years ago that it happened and Daddy's been dead for the last twenty-six. Every man has his Legacy.

Yes, well, moving on. Lots of your higher-class mo-tels back then had "Magic Fingers" on the beds. You put a quarter in the little box on the nightstand and the bed would commence to throb and vibrate so intensely it would rattle your fillings and make your nose itch. This would go on for about ten or fifteen minutes and then it would be time for another quarter. I cannot imagine how these ever fell out of favor and I think the fine folks in the hospitality industry would do well to consider staging a comeback.

Suffice it to say, Rhon and I were totally enamored of the Magic Fingers and we would require Daddy to supply us with piles of quarters to feed our insatiable desire for the shaking beds. These things were closely akin to the electric pony rides that were, at the time, stationed outside every grocery store in America. There was really no "ride" to it at all. The fake pony would simply quiver a bit and perhaps move an inch or so forward and back—hardly the thrill of a lifetime—and yet we were all driven quite insane by the manic desire to mount up that was enkindled in our young breasts at the very sight of them, and if our mothers EVER wanted to get home before botulism began growing in the bags of provisions, she was well advised to just cough up the damn nickel and wait the forty-five seconds while we rode the stupid pony.

The pony rides, as it turned out, were just a gateway drug for our generation. As so often happens, Rhon and I had had our pony-lust gratified so many times, we were hooked, and so naturally, as we grew older, we could no longer be satisfied with a little pony ride. (Also, we could no longer fit on them, but that's beside the point.) We graduated to the Magic Fingers bed and, of course—just like marijuana costs more than Mad Dog 20/20 and heroin costs more than hash—our habit went from a nickel every week to ten days, depending on how often Mama had to go to the store, to maybe fifty to seventy-five cents A NIGHT if we were in a room that had a Magic Fingers. I'm sure there's a Wayward Youth parable in here somewhere since, not speaking for Rhonda, I can however testify to the amount of money I was personally, in later years, to spend on vibrators. I'm just sayin' . . .

Anyway, one night we had arrived at our Holiday Inn for the night and had pleaded and cajoled our ration of quarters from Daddy, dropped one in the slot and stretched out, prepared to be at least shook and rattled if not necessarily rolled. Nothing happened. We put in another quarter—same zero result. We put in one more quarter and gave the box a resounding whack—which has always been the universally accepted and employed first-choice method for repairing any unresponsive mechanical device—it STILL did not work AND it now had three of our quarters.

Daddy was summoned. He, of course, had to personally put one more quarter in and give it his own man-sized whack just to be sure it was, in fact, not functioning properly. Satisfied that the unit was not only NOT going to perform, it was also NOT going to give back what had grown now to be a full dollar's investment, Daddy called the front desk and the manager promised to send someone up to attend to the matter promptly—which he did.

Our erstwhile bellboy returned to our room and gave the box a most serious looking-at. He stopped just short of stroking his nonexistent goatee and uttering a pensive "Hmmmmm," but I'm sure he thought of it. Instead, he picked up yet another one of OUR quarters and, before we could stop him, plunked it into the comatose machine and gave it his own authoritative whack, which produced exactly the same result that all previous coins and whackage had wrought. He then DID say, "Hmmmm," although with no accompanying chin-stroke, turned on his heel, and headed for the door, pausing only to speak those time-honored words that, in any language on earth, actually mean "You've seen the last of me, suckers" but nonetheless sound like "I'll be right back."

As we heard his footsteps moving languorously down the elevated walkway in front of our second-floor poolside room, the lack of any discernible urgency in that sound assured us that the bellboy would not be swiftly returning, if indeed, he ever did so at all. This did not sit well with the occupants of room 212, but only one of those occupants got an evil eye-gleam and headed for the car, chortling to himself, as he strode and then drove happily away.

He returned to the room a short time later carrying two things: one of them was a screwdriver. Instructing us to close the drapes, wait outside, and knock if anyone approached, the fiend set about his work. A few minutes later, he called us inside and told us, with a wicked cackle, to watch and say nothing. He called the front desk again and told the manager that we were still waiting for our Magic Fingers to be repaired and indicated that our patience was wearing thinner all the time.

Daddy could tell from the manager's tone that a good-sized fire would soon be lit under the slackass of a certain bellboy, and sure enough, in just a minute, there was a knock on the door. The bellboy had arrived with his own screwdriver and the threat of termination almost visibly hanging above his head. He set to work disassembling the Magic Fingers bedside box and Daddy could scarcely contain his gleeful self as the young man, tongue pressed between tight lips, feverishly fumbled with the screws.

At last all the stubborn screws were wrenched from their slots and the cover of the box came away. It would be hard to say which expression was worth more: the one on the face of the beleaguered bellboy who had just taken the cover off a recalcitrant Magic Fingers box and unbelievably and inexplicably discovered a large white fully intact hen egg sitting on top of a buck twenty-five's worth of quarters—or the face of the man who had just unbelievably and inexplicably PUT it there. I'd have to say both them faces were worth a whole lot more quarters' worth than that little box would hold.

Asset-Preserving Tip

Well, if I could, I'd give everybody a daddy just like mine—but I can't and I can't even loan you mine on account of he be done passed. All I can do is make you laugh by telling you about him—and hopefully inspire you to be for somebody what he was for me. The way to do that would be to be willing to play, anytime, anywhere—but also to be willing and able to see the humor in all things and just refuse to take ANY-thing too seriously, most importantly yourownself.

~12~

Security Level: Fuchsia

I know some folks who are as old or even older than I am who not only still have a lust for wandering but are still eager to indulge it. We don't hang out much. It is not an age-related development for me, however, that, aside from the fact that I am your basic homebody—no, I take that back—I am not the BASIC model at all—I am the superdeluxe KING-sized homebody—I don't want to go anywhere, ever, for any reason. I don't care what they got there, I don't want to see it. I want to be AT home, preferably on my back porch or out on the lake, ALL the time and I am not exaggerating—at all. I WILL go to church but only because Lelon Thompson sings like an angel and so does Baby Jan—it's worth the hour's drive to hear them. And Keith Tonkel does always manage to have the Word I was especially needing to hear that day, so fine, I don't mind listening to his preaching, scattered in amongst the singing.

And well, of course, I WILL go to the grocery store, but only because I love to cook and I love to eat even more than that. I actually enjoy going to get the groceries—it's putting them away that I despise. But anyway, church and groceries are really about the only two reasons for leaving my house that don't make me terminally crabby.

Please note that this is merely local travel, and I view and avoid even this as if it were plague-ridden. From that, it can be extrapolated that out-of-town travel sends me figuratively into orbit—since literal orbit would be waaaay too far from home.

At one time, I regarded the prospect of long car trips with the same enthusiasm I would feel for long prison sentences. It is therefore astounding to me that some person or persons unknown have somehow contrived to make driving twelve thousand (understand me: twelve THOUSAND) miles in a big giant RV with my husband and two (TWO) semilarge to enormous dogs seem like a DREAM COME TRUE when compared with even one short hop on an airplane to anywhere. You may as well just start hopping—as in up and down on the ground—and work your way to your destination—it'll be quicker and less stressful in the long run.

On my last two book tours, I did, in fact, travel by the aforementioned big giant RV—with the aforementioned spouse and canines—for the aforementioned twelve thousand actual road miles. The signing dates at the various bookstores around the country required our appearance in a different city every day for about forty days. At first thought, this seems like a delightful cross-country excursion with one's favorite beings, doesn't it?

And it would be, except for the fact that, when one is on a book tour, one must appear at the assorted stores when THEY want you and can fit you into THEIR schedule, and unfortunately, no matter who one is, one will not be the only one of one's ilk out there on a book tour and so one will inevitably run into scheduling conflicts and find one's self plunged into what is known in literary circles as "Book Tour Hell." And yes, that IS redundant.

While I cannot say that I have ever met an author who does not LOVE meeting and greeting his or her book-buying public—I have also never met one who does not visibly cringe at the words "book tour." This is because, while the events themselves are nothing but a pure de-light—what one has to go through to GET TO the events makes running barefoot through the various compartments of hell seem like park romping by comparison and one would willingly sign up for the run instead if one only knew how—and, of course, could be convinced that it would somehow sell a book.

When we first got word that my esteemed publishers, Mr. Simon and Mr. Schuster, would be sending me out and about the country via land-based travel in lieu of, shudder, flying both thither and yon, I, for one, was ecstatic. However, my enthusiasm for the prospect was pitifully pallid compared to the back-flipping display put on by my husband/business manager/

Cutest Boy in the World, Kyle Jennings—because, you see, HE was to be the Designated Driver of the Big-Ass Bus that, we were told, was approximately forty-three feet long and twelve and a half feet high. Two words: *Wet. Dream.*

Our dogs were equally thrilled at the prospect of two whole months of 24-7 togetherness with us, the Centers of Their Universe. Plus, lots of Cracker Barrels are involved and that always means "bacon for the dogs," so there was that added inducement for them.

What it meant to me personally was not having to unpack and repack a suitcase every single day for two months. It meant not surviving on nothing but minibar jellybeans and Pringles for sometimes days on end. It meant not having to origami my enormous frame into ever-shrinking airplane seats. No loud talkers, no screaming babies, no fucking PRETZELS. Is there a more irritating nonfood item than a pretzel? I think not. I can't think of anything that pisses me off more when I am starving than the proffer of a pretzel. But that's just me.

The most thrilling aspect to me of a nonflying book tour, though, was NO AIRPORT SECURITY. In just a few short years of existence, TSA has managed to do the impossible—they have surpassed the U.S. Postal Service in the employment of Persons Most Likely to Drive Other Persons Completely Insane.

I have, of course, the utmost respect and appreciation for the job at hand for both the post office and the transportation security folks—but you have to admit there are a disturbingly large number of dumbo apples in both barrels.

On Queen Ellyn's most recent trek to Jackson from the hinterlands of Oregon for the execution of her yearly Parade duties, she carelessly, stupidly, made a last-minute insertion into her carry-on bag of one of the most deadly threats known to our airways. How she could do such a thing and hope to get away with it is beyond me—I mean, it's not like the rules for airline safety are new or anything—we all know them, and if we don't, it doesn't matter because there are countless signs in the security areas of all airports outlining them, and, of course, there is the TSA designated hollerer at every station to remind us.

Let us not forget for an instant the tremendous dangers these rules are designed to protect us all from and let us not for an instant let down our guards or become lax in the enforcement of these rules, lest unspeakable disaster strike needlessly.

And yet. She brazenly attempted to slide this potential weapon of mass destruction undetected through security and BOARD AN AIRCRAFT with it. The dozens of other unsuspecting and totally innocent passengers who were compliant with all the rules had no idea that this small woman who appeared to be such a nice person was actually a sneak of the lowest, most cowardly form.

She looked like all of them—regular ole Amur-kin—no suspicious head gear or non-Anglo ethnicity—it just goes to show you—profiling is wrong. Imagine my surprise when I heard this story—this is a woman I have loved and welcomed not only into my home but aboard my very FLOAT! And yet. Here she was—attempting to subvert our NATIONAL SECURITY by concealing in her carry-on bag a fully loaded container of yogurt.

Luckily for all the other passengers with what could have been the grave misfortune of traveling on that particular day, through that particular airport—TSA was On the Job. The potential death cup was detected on the first pass through the X-ray machine and there was a great hue and cry throughout the area. "WHOSE BAG IS THIS? WHOSE BAG IS THIS?" Those in possession of firearms had their hands hovering inches above their weapons—ready to draw down on the culprit should he or she make a threatening move of any kind.

Ellyn, being slightly hard of hearing in crowded places, was not immediately aware that the jig was up on her little caper and she joined all the other passengers in looking around dazed and confused at what had set off the ire of the entire TSA staff, straining to catch sight of the villain and discern what crime against society had just been thwarted by the thankfully alert X-ray observer person.

"WHOSE BAG IS THIS WITH THE YOGURT IN IT? THERE IS A BAG HERE CONTAINING YOGURT—WHOSE BAG IS THIS? WHO DOES THIS YOGURT BELONG TO?"

Just as Ellyn realized it was her bag and her yogurt that was causing all the commotion in the bullpen, the name on the bag was deciphered by the code breaker on duty and the hunt narrowed. "PASSENGER ELLYN WEEKS! PASSENGER ELLYN WEEKS! WE HAVE YOUR BAG—CONTAINING YOGURT—IN THE SECURITY CHECK POINT—STEP OUT OF LINE IMMEDIATELY AND IDENTIFY YOURSELF TO THE OFFICERS! PASSENGER! ELLYN! WEEKS! COME FORWARD IMMEDIATELY—THERE IS YOGURT IN YOUR BAG!"

"Deer in the headlights" is the phrase that comes to mind as I imagine the shock and fear that must have registered on her face as she realized she had, in fact, been caught—her demonic deed uncovered and announced to the entire Sea-Tac Airport. She's an intelligent woman—to this day, I just can't imagine how she thought she would get away with it. The container CLEARLY says on all sides of the label, "EIGHT ounces." (And it does not matter if you eat most of it so it contains only the permitted THREE—if it says eight on the outside, it's eight on the inside, according to The Holy Book of Regulations. There MUST be strict enforcement of the three-ounce rule, because you just KNOW that SOMEbody will try to get by with five or six sooner or later, although not many would be as brazen as Ellyn—going for a full EIGHT-count.)

You think you know somebody and the next thing you know, this person you've called "friend" and trusted completely in every way just destroys your faith in most of humanity like this—just because SHE thought SHE might get "hungry" waiting for her plane and thought she might "save a few bucks" by bringing HER OWN yogurt with her—EIGHT full ounces of it, too—HIDDEN in her carry-on bag—and that would give HER the right to just thumb her little Anglo-Saxon button nose at the very fiber and foundation of our great nation—that being, of course, the rabid enforcement of inane regulations.

And I say that because when Ellyn finally did make good on her arrival at the Hilton Hotel in Jackson and she tiredly set about unpacking all her luggage—including the offending carry-on bag—imagine her surprise when she reached in to pull a mysterious object out of the bottom of the bag and what did she see in her hand when she gave it a final yank? A PAIR OF SHEARS WITH EIGHT-INCH BLADES.

She'd long forgotten what they were ever in there for—she just packed on top of them, unawares. Thank God they got so wound up over that YOGURT—she might have ended up on the airline's blacklist if they'da found them big-ass scissors.

Is That a Vibrator in Your Bag or Are You Just Glad to See Me?

Not only does one need to exercise extreme particularity when packing one's carry-on satchels, the current state of world affairs has necessitated or at least facilitated such unprecedented forays into our Private Matters that it also behooves one to reconsider one's choices in one of the Most Private of Our Matters, that being the selection of sex toys, specifically the items one wishes to carry with one, within one's checked baggage, when one is traveling on public conveyances.

Great care and caution should be employed in this selection process on account of everybody in the TSA is gonna be looking at it and fooling with it. So THINK about what all you put in that suitcase you check through to your destination. If one is traveling to a place that has access to normal electrical outlets, then might I suggest you choose a Plug-In Guy as opposed to a Battery-Operated Boyfriend?

For one thing, it's not going to LOOK at all "lifelike" and therefore it will be a much lesser source of entertainment for the bored inspectors—this works in your favor. And it also, obviously, must actually be plugged into a wall socket in order to, well, do what it do and so no bored inspector can decide to randomly flip its switch and say, just for grins, leave it running in your suitcase, which will not only put you at risk of arriving at your destination with dead batteries—woe is you—but also offers you the stellar opportunity to be summoned over the PA system throughout the EN-tire airport and commanded to return to the baggage security scan to account for the unexplained buzzing in your luggage.

Activating battery-operated vibrators in suitcases is apparently one of the top five favorite things for TSA agents to do, it seems—even more than loosening all the caps of the liquids in your makeup bag so everything in your suitcase gets perfumed and/or moisturized—after all, they don't get to BE THERE to

SEE when you discover THAT little trick. So with the live vibrator in the bag, you can be assured of an enthusiastic crowd gathering to witness your luggage inspection.

I'm Just a Businesswoman, Why Do You Ask?

I used to like to think I was providing some welcome diversion and entertainment for our overworked TSA personnel as they dutifully inspected my carry-on bag. Passing through thirty or forty different airports in as many days will cure one of any desire to have any sort of verbal exchange with them, however, and that is precisely the situation in which I currently find myself: the novelty, as they say, has worn plumb off.

For one thing, I am always flying in and out on different airlines—meaning I will have two months' worth of ONE-WAY tickets all over the country, so I am immediately Suspect in each of the respective airports. I am "randomly selected" for a more intensive examination every single time—coincidence? Likely. Fortunately, as yet, I have not been subjected to a full-body/cavity search, but I feel it's only a matter of time.

Close inspection of my carry-on bag is mandatory at every checkpoint because the X-ray immediately spots and alerts TSA to the big-ass crown in my bag. I have no idea what it looks like on their equipment but I'm sure it looks lethal—it's the size of the sun and extremely spiky. So, we go to the designated search area and they ask permission to open my bag and I give it—like, what choice do I have?—and they open it and they see, in person, the big-ass crown, and naturally, their simple basic human curiosity is piqued—but add to that the fact that they are gub'mint-related entities—well, they have Questions.

It used to be entertaining to try to explain myself to them, but as I said—I'm over that. So now when they drag out the big-ass crown and ask me what it's for, I just look bland and state the facts—"I'm The Sweet Potato Queen," like THAT explains ANYTHING. I don't offer anything further—answer only the questions asked. They look expectant for a moment, but when nothing else is forthcoming, they're so surprised, they can't think of any other pertinent queries and they move on, somewhat uncomfortably, to the remaining contents of my suspicious baggage. Whereupon they discover the presence of an enormous cache of bumper stickers reading, NEVER WEAR PANTIES TO A PARTY, which, you've got to admit, WOULD beg the question, no matter who you are. I stand erect, gazing fixedly at some point on the horizon, silent but inwardly chortling, knowing as I do, what they are going to discover NEXT.

They open the long thin cardboard box and they see the contents within: five thousand hot pink business-sized cards that say, "LICK YOU ALL OVER—10 cents—Ask about our other Specialties." And again, out of my own personal over-it-ness and, of course, in deference to all the other hapless passengers awaiting their own respective turns at the inspection table, I offer nothing in the way of explanation. I do freely admit to a gleeful sense of satisfaction at the thought of leaving discombobulated TSA personnel in my wake across the USA.

IS Dat You?

Many long years ago, when my daddy was still alive and traveling around on bidness, he and a male business associate got stuck in a small town due to an untimely automobile malfunction. It was particularly untimely because it occurred just after quitting time at the only mechanic's garage on a rainy afternoon on the day before some big local to-do.

This meant a couple of things to our travelers—namely, that the car wasn't going anywhere until at least midafternoon the following day, assuming the lone mechanic showed up for work and was in the mood to even attempt to fix their car and was also in possession of whatever part might be needed to do so.

It also meant that the one hotel in town was filled to something very like capacity—which never happened except once a year, for the big local to-do, whatever it was, that was scheduled for the very next day—so that when Daddy and his associate finally arrived, soaking wet from walking many, many blocks in the rain from the closed mechanic's shop, Daddy was greatly disheartened to learn that there might also be a problem concerning any overnight accommodations for them.

Daddy asked the desk clerk/owner of the hotel for two rooms and was told that there was only one room left in the whole establishment but it did have two beds in it and Daddy said fine, he'd take it, and thus began the check-in process.

The first snag was Daddy wanted to write a check to pay for the room and his driver's license was in the glove box of the broken-down car, many, many rain-soaked blocks away. When the clerk asked for identification and was told that the license was in the car—many, many rain-soaked blocks away—there was reluctance on his part to accept the out-of-town check. He reiterated that he needed some proof of identity. As it happened, there was a large mirror hanging on the wall behind the desk, and Daddy leaned to one side so that he could look around the desk clerk and see his own reflection in it. He studied it for a long moment and then gestured for the desk clerk to turn around and look, and he asked the clerk, "Is that a mirror?" The clerk, of course, said yes, it IS—his tone indicating a level of irritated incredulity that there could be any question about what it was—it was OBVIOUSLY a mirror. Daddy said, "I thought so. Let me get a good look here," and he gazed thoughtfully for another long moment, saying, "Hmmmm, well, then, YEP, that's ME, all right."

Okay, so the ID problem was solved, but a particularly thorny issue still remained: there was only one room—and the desk clerk was just learning that there were two MEN wanting to book it. Even though there WERE admittedly two beds in that room—the owner of this small-town establishment was not prepared, in 1962, to be renting out one of HIS rooms for two MEN to share, regardless of any broken-down-car-in-the-pouring-ass-rain-closed-mechanic's-garage-type circumstances. Looked like a Queer Deal to him and he wudd'n taken NO-O-O-O chances of any of THAT happening at HIS ho-tel, no-sirree-bobtail-cat. (Now, there's a Southernism I've never understood, although I've lived here my EN-tire life. I get the no-sirree part—but what does the bobtail cat signify? Anybody out there know? Anybody?)

Anyway, the bidness associate had been wandering around, checking out the cool old hotel lobby, and was unaware of the checking-in problems and that he might soon be relegated to sleeping in the broken-down car many, many rain-soaked blocks away. He totally missed the whole ID-by-mirror episode and was just approaching from some distance when the Homosexshull Problem was being hinted at.

The clerk had asked, as they used to do, who would be sharing the room, and Daddy had indicated his wandering business associate and the clerk had just begun protesting the disturbing impropriety of it all. So all the business associate heard as he walked up was Daddy inexplicably describing HIM as "Oh, no, sir, it's not what you think—that's just my idiot brother-in-law. I'm taking him back to my wife's parents, somebody has to watch him all the time or he gets nekkid and shits in the street—but I'll give him his medicine and he'll sleep all night, don't you worry."

Luckily, the business associate had the presence of mind to infer from hearing that colorful if confusing description of his veryownself that there must be some kind of very good reason for it and so he kept his mouth shut—which did require retrieving his lower jaw from the floor, to which it had no doubt dropped as he heard himself so described. And so he was able to sleep in a semicomfy hotel bed that night, as opposed to a not-so-sumptuous car seat, and although everyone talked very slowly and with a little more than necessary volume to him—as if he were not only mentally deficient but also slightly hard of hearing—they were all pretty nice. Daddy was regarded as quite the saintly figure for the good care taken of his "handicapped brother-in-law," so I suppose it comes under the all's-well-that-ends-well clause.

Well, today, of course, nobody cares with whom you share your room, but even an attempt at self-identification by way of a MIRROR would probably get you arrested in some areas—airports, for example. I can't believe we have to have a PASSPORT even to go to Canada and Mexico now. Bummer.

Back in our salad days—why do they call 'em that? We never ate salads then and we certainly wouldn't consider salad a positive, unless it was maybe 'tater salad made with tons of mayo and crispy bacon—that would be swell, so okay, in that context, we can accept "salad days" as a good thing—SO, back in ours— me and my sister, Judy, would run down to Cozumel at the drop of a hat or anything else—often we would go when nothing at all had been dropped—we just looooved it there and it was so easy and cheap, we could hardly afford to stay HOME.

We had found ourselves in possession of (or is it possessed by?) one of those oft-touted wild hairs and were upping to take off and head for the island without a whole lot of advance preparation. I had thrown some stuff in a duffel bag and driven to New Orleans so that we could fly outta there early the next morning.

Somehow, in the discussion of what all we were collectively packing or leaving, it became known to us that I had run off to N.O. without bringing any form of acceptable border-crossing identification. At that time, you could use a passport, of course, or you could use your voter registration card (even though there was no such thing as voter ID then) or you could use what was called an "affidavit of citizenship," which was a notarized piece of paper saying that you were who you were and you lived at such-and-such a place in the United States and that you were, in fact, a citizen of same. No photo, just a notary's signature. Pretty solid proof of, well, nothing.

I didn't own a passport, and since my voter's registration card was not in my wallet where I thought it was, there was no telling where it actually was, and besides, I really was NOT in the mood to drive the three hours BACK to Jackson, spend however many hours it would take to try to locate the card, and then drive the three more hours back to New Orleans in order to be at the airport for our early flight to Cozumel.

And so, at around nine PM, after a few cocktails, we settled on crafting for me an affidavit of citizenship. It was amazingly easy. We simply went down to Judy's office and typed up the requisite wordage, found her boss's notary seal, applied it to the paper in the proper place, made sure we had the two necessary "witness signatures"—which, I'm not sure, I think we may have signed ourownselves and then, after all this chicanery, for some unknowable reason, Judy weaseled at this juncture and could not bring herself to add the actual forgery of her boss's signature on the seal to our list of crimes, and so around midnight, as I recall, we hunted him down at a bar and got him to sign it, without reading it, of course. And that piece of worthless paper was all I needed to guarantee my exit from and reentry into this country that I do so love.

I miss those days. I suppose my still-underage daughter has some degree of understanding for the pleasant thrill associated with dancing around government regulations—Lord knows how many fake IDs she's had confiscated in recent years. But, while there will always be SOME-body from whom a truly dedicated minor will be able to procure alcohol—border crossings have gotten a tad bit trickier, not to mention, like, totally vital. I mean, not for any amount of refreshing tequila-laced beverages consumed watching any number of sunsets on any pristine but foreign beaches would I want to get STUCK somewhere OUT-SIDE the US of A and not be able to get back IN.

Tips for Trouble-Free Travel

No matter what your age and/or station in life, I actually have only one travel tip for you: DON'T DO IT.

This works for me. After much study of this problem of travel-related woes, I have found that as long as I am sitting on my back porch—or lolling in my tub—I spend zero dollars per gallon for gas, I am literally unaffected by commute times and/or traffic snarls, I don't worry about what to pack—too little? too much?—I am affected only by the weather if the wind is blowing rain from the south, in which case I get dampened on the porch and must take to the tub unless I am already in the tub, in which case the weather does not matter.

Airport security bothers me not at all—new and more stringent regulations do not affect my plans—I can make pipe bombs on my back porch if I decide I want to and someone shows me how—but I have only very simple plans, which are to sit and mouth-breathe while staring at water, whether in the lake or in the tub.

I don't care how small the seats have gotten or that there is sufficient leg and head room only for individuals five feet tall and under.

No one ever tries to make me eat pretzels.

My skin is not turned to thin, powdery leather by the negative humidity in a hotel room.

I am never awakened at some ridiculous hour by the bedside alarm inconsiderately left set by the previous room's occupant, who had to get up in order to arrive at the airport the prescribed six or eight hours in advance of a (delayed or canceled) flight.

If I choose to dine on Pringles and old jelly beans, it's because I'm home alone and lazy—not because delayed flights meant that I arrived at my hotel long after room service shut down and I thought I would surely die if I didn't ingest some form—any form—of calories immediately.

My credit cards are never in any danger of being either stolen or declined.

The restrooms are as clean as I want them to be and there is no wait to use them.

I don't ever go out to sit on the porch only to be told—either by a hard-to-read blue screen or a nearly impossible-to-understand bellowing voice on the PA system—that my sitting-down place has been changed and that now I must go to the other side of the lake and that the train that would normally take me there is malfunctioning so there will be a "short" walk involved in the relocation process.

Any and all travel-related problems can be easily averted with this one simple step: stay home. It works beautifully for me and I recommend it to you most highly.

~13~

Onward, Through the Fog

January and February of each year finds me running all over the country, hawking my latest book—a brutal task but not without its benefits, the primary one of those being the opportunity to meet and visit, up close, with all manner of Queens. This gives me the chance to hear, firsthand, your own personal tales of your own journeys into Queenliness, and it is just the most gratifying and reassuring thing in the world to me—to see the Queendom ever growing and the Queens themselves growing ever wiser.

For example, I learned that Queen Crystal is enjoying peaceful sleep, night after night, undisturbed by any free-floating fears about the away-from-home-supervision conduct of her teenage daughter Meg. Here's why: our little Meggie loves to cook and she's always in the kitchen trying new recipes, which often call for ingredients that Queen Crystal does not keep readily on hand. One creation called for Parmigiano Reggiano, of which there was none in the house, and so off the two went to the grocery store together to secure the necessary provisions. As long as she was there and walking RIGHT BY the beer and wine section, QC thought it was as good a time as any to sample the newest flavor of wine coolers, and so she snagged a six-pack. Meg was off on the cheese hunt and did not, therefore, witness the wine cooler selection.

Okay, so they're in the checkout line and the little checker girl scans the wine coolers through the register and asks to see QC's proof of age (always thrilling to those of us of a certain age), but when she made this request, she was holding up the CHEESE. QC joked, "Wow, getting carded for CHEESE! What next?" and Meg looked astounded. "You got carded for CHEESE?" "It's imported," QC said, without missing a beat.

As they walked to the car, Meg was clearly processing the moment, and as they got in the car, she asked her mama, "How old do I have to BE before I can buy that cheese?" Hmmm . . . and thus, Queen Crystal sleeps in heavenly peace.

I'm told that Queen Pat's parents slept well during her teenage years as well, although they certainly should not have. This was one of those blissful-ignorance situations and nobody would EVER have been the wiser, except, of course, for the fact that—like so many of us—Pat has herself a big-mouth buddy— by the name of Laura. (Yours may have another name, but a big mouth by any other name will naturally blab just as much.)

What Pat did and got away with that Laura is now blabbing

is this: as a teenager, Pat found herself on a pretty tight parental curfew leash, and she was instructed not only to be in at what she deemed to be a ridiculously early hour for one as trustworthy and mature as she (snort), but she was also to briefly waken her parents upon her home arrival to confirm that she was, in fact, safe in the coop by the witching hour.

While still out on the town in full carouse mode, she would note that her curfew time was fast approaching. A few minutes before she was due in, she would take herself to a quiet spot and phone home. A sleepy parent would fumble for the bedside phone and mutter a muffled hello—whereupon Pat would quickly say, "It's okay, it's for me—I just walked in the door—sorry the phone woke you"—AS IF she had just answered the phone in another part of the house—when IN FACT, she was merely pausing in her debauchery miles and miles away. Sleepy Mom and/or Dad would look at the clock and hang up the phone in annoyance at being awakened thusly, but most of all, just relieved at the knowledge that their little angel Pat was safe in the nest once more. And the little hellion would go right on partying until she and the cows decided it was time to come home, and she would slip in—undetected.

If, as you read this, you're still young enough to be living at home and adhering to a curfew—you should be aware that YOUR MOTHER CAN READ and so this tactic, if you were thinking of employing it, has just been removed from your arsenal of trickery. If you're the kid—sorry. If you're the mom—you're welcome.

I've Searched the World Over

And learned this for certain: The Secret to a Happy Marriage . . . remains a secret. Suffice it to say that while LOVE may, in fact, be BLIND, marriage is NOTHING if not an eye-opener. Boy-hidee—is it ever! Do y'all ever read the newspaper advice columns of Carolyn Hax? I adore her—I think she is just ate up with good ole COMMON SENSE and that, coupled with a mighty fine turn of phrase, makes her worthy of our attention and praise. Somebody wrote in once and asked her what she thought was a "good age" at which to get married. Ms. Hax responded that the "good age" would be the one at which you find somebody so good for you that spending your life with him would be a natural extension of who you are—which SEEMS like SUCH a simple answer, doesn't it?

She went on with the tricky part—that being that FIRST you have to be mature enough to KNOW who YOU ARE—which, unfortunately, is too often clear only in hindsight—or, worse, full-on delusion. Immaturity and bad choices CAN be caught early, according to Queen Carolyn—IF we are ready to see it—in arguments we have with ourselves and/or others about how mature we are or how great our potential mate really is. OOOOH, she is soooo smart.

As a semigeezer gearing up to hand over the world to the next generation, I am greatly heartened by a delightful missive I received from one of my very favorite little Larva Queens,

Alexis. First of all, Alexis considers my dear friend Marlyn Schwartz and me to be veritable fonts of wisdom—which I think indicates a pretty fair share of wisdom in her own young self—and she states that betwixt us, Marlyn and I have helped her on more than one occasion as she fumbles her way through her twenties, and we are gratified to hear it.

We are further gratified to learn that little Queen Alexis has started a rebel faction in the very midst of her local Junior League. Don't those very words give you a little thrill? A REBEL FACTION in a JUNIOR LEAGUE! It is rare that one is privileged to witness such raw courage in one so young. It seems that after some discussion with the dozen or so other Single Members in the League, Alexis determined that they had all grown just a bit tired of hearing, repeatedly, from the MARRIED membership, "You're still SINGLE? That is a SIN!" Ostensibly this is meant as a sort of compliment to the single one, indicating that she is just so obviously completely and totally FABULOUS in every way, it is just a SIN for her to be "going to waste" as an unmarried person—but it sorta stops feeling complimentary after about the 438th time one hears it about one's fabulous self.

Thus, Alexis rallied her little band of "spinsters" and dubbed them "The Upside of Sin" and declared herself Benevolent Dictator for Life—to which the other girls had no objection because Alexis is a consummate party planner and they knew they would be in very fun hands. By the end of the first meeting,

Alexis had already announced the party schedule for the upcoming year, which would include the Bridesmaid Retirement Party, the Beware the Ides of March celebration, as well as other festivities to commemorate any and all perhaps lesser-known holidays, such as September 2, which, you may be unaware, is National Beheading Day, and even though we are not sure in what COUNTRY that is a national holiday—we have our suspicions, of course—nonetheless, it clearly calls for cocktails, no?

Alexis further decided but with unanimous support that whenever one of the Upsiders did get married, the group would throw a funeral for her. They would all wear slenderizing black cocktail dresses and celebrate the end of the life of a fabulous single girl—complete with eulogies—and gorge themselves on time-honored funeral foods from the appropriate sweet, salty, fried, and au gratin food groups.

I feel a welcome sense of relief as I read any e-mails from Alexis—that we have somehow managed to impart worthy ideals to at least ONE young woman, and it makes it just a little bit easier for me to contemplate retirement—knowing that we are in at least ONE pair of capable hands.

Okay, make that TWO—because an e-mail from Queen Christen has just come to me and caused me to wonder if the Nobel committee would consider offering a prize for Most Diabolical Divorce-Related Revenge Tactics. If so, Christen is a mortal lock for this year's award.

She left the SOS (sack of shit) right after obtaining a restraining order—which the good folks in the ER, where she'd spent the previous night, helped her get right quick-like—and when she left him, she also magnanimously left in his possession ALL the televisions in the house—without even so much as a hint of a demand from the SOS that she do so. She just did it out of the unbearable sweetness of her soul. But then, out of that OTHER part of her soul, she TOOK every single REMOTE CONTROL with her—bwahahahaha!

Furthermore, it seems that, throughout their ill-fated marriage, the SOS had clung with demonic ferocity to a pair of decades-old deerskin slippers that looked and smelled like roadkill, and whenever he would misplace them, she would be viciously accused of having some responsibility for their disappearance. She knew that if, as a parting gesture, she were to dispose of them, he would know instantly that she had done it, and she feared the consequences would too far outweigh the satisfaction, and so she just took ONE.

Whenever she felt glum for any reason over the next year or so, she had only to call up the mental picture of him tearing the house apart—over and over and over again—looking for those remotes and that one ratty-ass slipper—and presto change-o! The dark clouds rolled away and she felt all sunny inside once more. It IS, after all, the simple things in life that really count.

I am thrilled nearly but not quite beyond words to report that just a few short years later, Christen met up with a lovely

young man from Memphis who, on their first Christmas together as a couple, gave her a complete set of Sweet Potato
Queen books. Of course, she married him and we are so certain
they are living happily EVER after.

And THEN, I was further gratified to hear from Queen
Sheryl that, after ten years of marriage, her first husband ran off
with her hairdresser, and frankly, it took Sheryl quite some time
to get over it. I mean, how would YOU feel? We all know how
hard it is to find a good hairdresser.

After the ensuing divorce, the hairdresser-stealing ex would
come pick up the kids for a visit on Sunday morning and return
them on Sunday evening. Whenever he brought them back, he
would actually come into the house and, in a seemingly off-
handed manner, just sort of saunter to the back of the house
and peek into Sheryl's bedroom. He was no longer interested in
occupying it hisownself but was nonetheless way too interested
in seeing if anybody else was. This was a source of irritation to
Sheryl and so she Took Steps.

The next Sunday, as soon as he left with the kids, she went
to work. She tangled the bedsheets and threw the throw pillows
across the room. She burned incense, drew the blinds, put a
pink scarf over a lamp with a low-watt bulb, put two wine-
glasses on the nightstand (with a few drops of Kool-Aid in the
bottom of each), put soft music on the stereo, threw a pair of
panties and a bra on the floor, made two distinct head prints on

one of the bed pillows, and then she went next door and BOR-
ROWED a FULL ashtray from her neighbor—which she placed
on her headboard above the bed.

And then she rested, although it must be said she was too
excited to nap. FINALLY, the hairdresser-stealing ex returned
with the kids. She immediately engaged the children in a lively
discussion in the kitchen, to give him plenty of leeway to mean-
der down the hall for his routine observation run. She stood
where she could watch him without being seen. She said he
gently pushed open the bedroom door and glanced in—clearly
expecting to see nothing but the normally perfectly ordered
room he was accustomed to viewing and, WHOA-NELLY! He
nearly tripped over his own jaw when he saw the Evidence. She
was gleeful.

As he approached the kitchen, she asked the kids, in her
sweetest Mommy voice, "Did you guys have a good time today?"
and while they were assuring her that, yes, ma'am, they sure
did—he walked in and said, "Well! Did MOMMY have a good
time today?" Winking, she said, "Oh, you bet!" knowing he
wouldn't be able to leave it at that—and she was right. He then
said, "So, was it anybody I know?" and without so much as a
pause, she said, perky as you please, "Hell, no! It wasn't even
anybody I know!"

Sheryl says, to this day, it was the best orgy she never had.
Sometimes, I swear, all IS right with the world, isn't it?

~14~

Still Men— After All These Years

First, of course, they are BOYS, and all evidence indicates that it's a case of early onset approximately 100 percent of the time. Once upon a time, in the little town of West Point, Georgia—which is the only place in the universe that I know about where one can get crispy-fried black-eyed peas, and that is at the Heart of the South Tea Room (which also has THE finest Southern cooking anywhere on the planet)—so it is worth going there if for no other reason than that—just to experience the miracle of the black-eyed peas, which are like salted peanuts only peas and nobody can figger out quite how they do it and they ain't tellin' so you just have to go there if you want some—there lived three little boy-type brother boys.

By boy-type boys, I mean the kind that're just as full of their own boyness as they could possibly be without busting wide open. Just so BAD, you could pinch their heads off—if they weren't so dang funny about it.

Okay, so Mom is driving them to school one morning and they are all buckled up in the backseat. The one in the middle announces that he is experiencing that happy-boy thing—the hard-on—and he is, in fact, quite happy about it and is equally happy to share the glad tidings with his fellow passengers. Brother-to-the-left gives a cursory glance in the direction of Middle brother and says, hmph, yeah, looks like you do, and goes back to staring out the window. Brother-to-the-right does not even look in Middle brother's direction but maintains his steady window gaze, but nonchalantly says, "Yeah, when I get a hard-on out in public, I usually just tuck it up under my belt."

This at first seems to Middle brother to be a most excellent—indeed brilliant—solution to what could be a troubling matter—since he, too, often found that he would be visited by the hard-on fairy at public and therefore inopportune moments—and his face kinda lit up at the suggestion momentarily. Just as quickly, his expression turned to confusion and then consternation as he processed the entire equation and realized that either his pants were too high or his equipment was too short for him to avail himself of this fine remedy.

If the smug faces on Left and Right brothers did not betray their treachery, their ensuing guffaws certainly did, as Mom just watched it all in her rearview mirror, thinking to herself what mean little shits they were—but she still laughed.

Phase Two

I'll grant you, they do walk a bit more upright these days and the prehensile tails seem to have vanished so, yes, they have become Men, but it would seem to me that there have not been any real discernible upgrades to the product in the last several thousand years.

Queen Jamie told me she'd been reading the online personal ads and came across this one that some igmo had posted: I am lowering MY standards so that YOU can RAISE YOURS. Where was he listed? In the Unmitigated Gall section? And how many affirmative responses do you reckon he got with THAT plum of a come-on?

Another one that we can't imagine working for 'em: "I'm a real catch—I've been to jail but never to prison." Oh, hey—can't let HIM get away! Can you even imagine—if that's the best thing that he can think of to say about HIMSELF?

If you've read any or all of my previous books—and, of course, you know that I fervently hope that you have or will— you know that I have talked at some length about the ever-astounding igmonosity constantly plaguing men—and by association, also women. To the best of my recollection, I believe that if not all, then certainly by far and away the majority, of my rants have been concerning igmos of the heterosexual male persuasion.

I guess, in my mind, homosexual males are either above or somehow exempt from overt acts of male-pattern stupidity. Once again, I have had a lesson in Just How Wrong I Can Be.

Queen Maria has been married and divorced four times herownself and she has blocked out most of those memories—keeping only enough of them handy to avert altar trip #5—but she has a bestest buddy who is a gay man who is, according to my research, the first documented Gay Igmo on record. The QueenBoy first of all went and married a woman—which is a total igmo thing for a gay man to do. They did ultimately divorce, of course, but THEN—here is the REAL igmo part of it—HE MARRIED HER AGAIN. We can only surmise that the fool just loooves to have a wedding. We can't imagine WHAT in the world SHE'S thinking.

But anyway, it doesn't even stop THERE. It seems that Queen-Boy also drinks a bit on occasion—no, that's not completely accurate—it seems that QueenBoy drinks a bit MUCH on occasion. It also seems that QueenBoy likes to SIT in his TRUCK and listen to the radio while he drinks a bit much. (Okay, he's not only an igmo gay man—he's a REDNECK igmo gay man—what next? Does he at least listen to show tunes on the radio?)

So, the other night, he sat in his truck, in the dark, drinking vats of beer, singing along with the radio, and he sat and drank and sang until he got sleepy, but when he decided he'd be better off passing out inside the house—he made the understandably alarming discovery that HE COULD NOT MOVE.

In a complete state of panic, he decided that he had consumed so much beer as to induce a stroke in his brainpan, so he did what any normal, clear-headed, right-thinking, married-but-gay drunk man would do when he realized he was paralyzed in his own truck in his own driveway in the dark—he called his best friend, Maria.

Maria, already getting in her car and speeding the few blocks to his house, said that she would, of course, come to his aid but that 911 MUST also be called and trained emergency personnel MUST be summoned. He whined that he didn't want to call them because he was in his UNDERWEAR and he didn't want them to see him.

They were still arguing about calling/not calling 911 when she wheeled up behind his truck, leaping out of her car before it was fully stopped, heart in her throat, raced over, yanked open his door, and discovered the source of his "paralysis." He was WEARING HIS SEATBELT.

So it would seem, gay or straight, makes no difference: we STILL can't make nothin' but a Man out of 'em and I don't care who he is, when we get 'im home, there's something BAD WRONG with him. However, that being said, there also has not been found a reasonable substitute for them and so we must continue to make do with what we've got, and thankfully, we're fairly happy with it most of the time.

It's not for lack of TRYING, however—all manner of Man Substitutes are available in the marketplace, many of them shockingly anatomically correct, while others are inexplicably styled to look like small woodland creatures. Others are not primarily designed to be battery-operated boyfriends at all, but Necessity is, after all, a Mother, isn't she?

Oh, yeah—Queen Tammy went on a Girl Trip to Hawaii with a whole bunch of her grown-up women friends—no Larva allowed—and, as will happen quite often over cocktails, the subject of BOBs came up for a lively discussion. Pros and cons of all manner of apparati were talked over at great length until one woman spoke up and said it was just silly to clutter up the house with a lot of superfluous equipment when one common household tool can do dual duty and can be left sitting out in plain sight in even the most conservative homes.

She was not allowed to speak again for several moments as they all, at once, tried to guess what this device that was both handy and dandy could possibly be. There was unanimous jaw-droppage when she allowed as how the ELECTRIC TOOTH-BRUSH made a perfectly FINE boyfriend—you just had to remember to apply the back, not the bristles, and also to have a Designated Brush for Alternate Duty.

You won't find this in the owner's manual, of course, but you have to admit, it does seem brilliant—dazzling smile AND

Something to Smile About—talk about your twofer! And here I thought it was smart to figure out you could use a regular ole manual-style toothbrush on your eyebrows—clearly a case of Not Thinking Big Enough.

Okay, Once in a While, It Does Happen

"It" being that one of US, meaning females, does something that qualifies us for a pretty high ranking on the Igmo Scale. Let me qualify that—we are quite often—way too often—guilty of committing gross igmonosities in our choice of MEN and in the resulting relationships with them—but in just regular ole day-to-day-living-type stuff, I don't think we are quite as prone to doing your basic random stupid shit as some others, namely, guys, are—BUT, as I said, once in a while, it does happen.

It happened once at the Michigan State Fair, where a nameless young Queen was strolling through the agriculture display building, along with her buddies—some of whom were boys, some of whom were girls; it is neither known nor relevant whether any of them were both. At any rate, the group of young ne'er-do-wells was, as I said, strolling, and they chanced upon an enormous fiberglass cow, as one is wont to do on occasion while strolling through an agriculture display, and often when one does make such a chance encounter, one is tempted to mount the beast—simply because, as they say, it is THERE.

And so it came to pass that our young and hapless Queen was herself stricken with what proved to be an overwhelming, albeit inexplicable, desire to clamber up on top of the big giant fake cow, which, as it turned out, was not quite as sturdy as she appeared to the casual observer to be. And so it was that our young and very-soon-to-be utterly-without-hap Queen used all the grace and skill she'd acquired in all the years of dance and gymnastics classes her parents worked so hard to pay for—and somehow managed to pull herself way up high—on the back of the really big giant cow. Just as she was beginning to catch her breath and really enjoy waving regally to her friends, who looked so tiny down there on the ground, so very far beneath her, there was a startling development cow-wise. It seems that Bossy was not really designed to be a load-bearing bovine, and after just a few short moments of supporting our young hap-deprived Queen, Bossy's back sort of opened up and, well, swallowed our friend.

Her friends, who, it seems, were no friends a-tall—had just been watching her with a mixture of misguided pride and envy, way up there on the big giant cow, and then POOF! She was gone—vanished before their very eyes, which were, truth be told, having just a leetle trouble focusing by this point anyway. They couldn't see the top of the cow so they had no idea that a great cow crater had formed and devoured their friend—it appeared to them that she had simply vanished. I'm quite certain there were more than a few mystified "Whoa, dudes!" exchanged before it was decided that the group should go. Not so much for help as for more beer—they didn't really see how anybody could help with this—nobody even knew the proper authority to notify in case of a person's disappearance from the top of a big giant cow—but luckily, somebody did know where there was beer to be had and so it was decided that leave should be taken in pursuit of beer and possibly burgers—looking at the big giant cow having reminded them that they were hungry.

And so off they went and the lonely cow-girl was forgotten. Not silent, though. It didn't take her long to ascertain that she was, in fact, buried alive inside a big giant cow and that she was furthermore trapped and unable to free herself from her oxlike ossuary, but she knew she and her worthless cohorts weren't the ONLY people touring the ag building that evening— somebody else was BOUND to come to gaze at big giant cow— and who knows—perhaps even be moved to climb it and discover the bottomless pit into which she had fallen. In any event, she figured sooner or later somebody surely would get close enough to hear her hollering—which she was doing a lot of—from inside the cow.

By and by, some folks did happen by and hear her pitiable cries for help, but they could not discern from whence the pleas were issued—no damsel in distress could be detected in the area. Of course, it never occurred to them that there might be a live girl trapped in the belly of the big giant cow—who could blame them, what are the odds of finding a live girl in such a place?—and it never occurred to her to offer hints as to her location. The cow belly apparently being the equivalent of a soundproof booth, she could not hear her would-be rescuers asking that most pertinent of all questions, "WHERE THE HELL ARE YOU?" And thus, she just lay in the bowels of the bovine, wailing, "HELP ME! HELP ME!" over and over, until she began to sound like a large cat meowing, and the folks started to think maybe that's what it was—just a big cat outside or on the roof or something.

They were beginning to get thirsty and hungry as well, but just as they started to head for the beer tent, an officer in the State Department of Natural Resources happened by, looking all official in his uniform, and so the folks stopped him and advised him that they thought they were hearing somebody yelling for help—but now they thought maybe it was a big cat, what did he think, and he stopped to listen in his official capacity.

As he did so, he put one hand on the side of the cow, to sort of lean against her for support while he was officially listening to officially determine if the sound was being made by a person or a big cat, and as he did so, his ring made a "thunk" against the cow's leg—a sound that could be heard by our prisoner, and upon hearing it, she renewed her frantic cries with great gusto and also with key information added: "HELP ME! HELP ME! I'M IN THE COW! I'M . . . IN . . . THE . . . CO-O-O-OW!"

Like THAT made any sense. Nobody believed it for a good few minutes but she stuck to her line—"Help me, help me, I'm in the cow, I'm IN THE CO-O-O-OW"—until the DNR guy finally radioed for somebody to "Come to the big giant cow and bring a ladder."

Like THAT made any sense. But he apparently was a high-ranking officer and had enough clout that a radio message from him demanding a ladder be brought to the big giant cow was met with compliance on account of presently, somebody did show up at the cow with a ladder, whereupon someone else was ordered up the ladder, and upon reaching the top, a girl-swallowing gap could be seen. Plus you could hear her hollering pretty good from up there.

And so, after much debate about methodology, a rescue team was assembled and our little Jonah-girl was extracted from the belly of the beast. It is not known if she went thence to Ninevah or if she had to pay for the cow, but she did have a beer and decided she definitely needed some new friends.

Asset-Preserving Tip

In the whole entire history of people climbing up on big giant fake cows and falling through the top and getting stuck inside for hours and hours and finally having to be cut out by trained rescue person-nel—NOT A SINGLE ONE OF THE TRAPPED CLIMBERS WAS DETER-MINED TO BE SOBER AT THE TIME OF THE INCIDENT. Possibly something to consider before happy hour, I'm just sayin'.

～15～

Give Me a Wham!
Give Me a Bam!

Then, and only then, may you give me a "Thank you,
MA'AM!" Somewhere around the time that we go from
thongs and stilettos to pillowcases with leg holes and black
Merrell sandals, we also go from cute girls to ma'ams. And it is
most unsettling.

We really don't mind the conversion to comfy clothing, but
being relegated to the Ma'am Section does not have the same
soothing effect on our psyches. The first time you get called
"Ma'am" by some young man you were just thinking was a
cutie-pie, well, your psyche will be singularly unsoothed, I can
promise you that. You will be ALL rumpled up in spirit, border-
ing closely on disgruntlement, I'd say.

I read a letter in an advice column from one just such rumpled-up, disgruntled woman who had been recently christened a ma'am by a man she didn't think was sufficiently younger than herself so as to warrant such a distinction and she was horrified. I'm not certain what relief she expected to get from the columnist, but the response printed would not have been much salve for my own soul so I doubt seriously that Angelina from St. Paul was much consoled either.

Apparently, the appalling appellation had been so shocking to Angelina from St. Paul that it forced to the forefront of her consciousness that all of a sudden she was forty-five years old and trapped in a body that featured a striking re-creation of her own mother's butt. Angelina was not having a good day.

The advice giver was clearly about twelve years old and I hope she's saving all her columns so she can go back and do the written equivalent of biting her tongue when she is on the other side of fifty and looks back at some of her answers.

The little Larva columnist wrote her—and they printed it in the paper—that getting older was nothing more than a "new and more interesting phase" and that she should celebrate her new curves and also be happy that some young people in the world still have good manners.

All us old women can tell her that it is "new and interesting" in much the same vein that waking up to a sky raining frogs and discovering that you and the world at large had suddenly been hit with a plague of boils would also be "new and interesting."

We can tell her that waking up to the discovery that you

have your mama's butt cannot, with a straight face or a glad heart, be described and dismissed as "new curves." That would be like the Weather Channel telling the folks in the path of a Cat 5 hurricane, "Nice breeze today and surf's up!" (Which they have never done, by the way.) Everybody knows you can't improve on impending doom by saying sweet things about it—with the one notable exception of this advice columnist, obviously.

OF COURSE there are still young people in the world with good manners—they're from THE SOUTH, hel-lo? Instilling and insisting on good manners is one of the things we do best and consistently, and part of that program is calling EVERY-BODY of ANY AGE "Sir" or "Ma'am," as is deemed appropriate by the apparent gender of the person to whom we are speaking. Occasionally, we encounter a "Pat-type" person whose gender is not readily discernible from a casual distance and we are forced to make a wild guess—and in those cases, there is a fifty-fifty chance we will guess right. There is a momentary awkwardness, of course, when we guess WRONG, but we are compelled to assign every human either a "ma'am" or a "sir" in direct conversation with them, so risks must be taken and any unfortunate consequences just have to be dealt with after the fact.

What Angelina wanted and needed to hear from the columnist was, "WHAT? He called YOU 'Ma'am'?! The very idea! Why, you don't look a day over twenty-seven! Clearly, he was just being overly polite and he prolly says that to every female in the world, just 'cause his mama told him to. And you do NOT have your mama's butt—you have a perfect little butter bean of a butt back there—what are you talking about?"

The main problem in that situation is plain to everybody who was reared in the South—the plaintiff was from Minnesota, the guy who uttered the offensive "Ma'am" was clearly from somewhere Southern, and the adviser was from New York. So only ONE person in this trio REALLY knew what was going on.

Our good friend and fellow author Bobby Cole (*The Dummy Line,* Context Publishing Company, 2008) is admittedly a FEW years younger than I am—who isn't, besides God and Ann-Margret?—but he is not THAT much younger, you know what I mean? And yet despite all my protestations to the contrary, he INSISTS on calling me "Mizz Jill." I do think perhaps that's worse than Ma'am. Ma'am at least can be passed off as a generic term of politeness; when they tack a "Mizz" or "Miss" on the front of your first name, it's PERSONAL. I have finally solved the problem, though—I just call HIM "MR. BOBBY."

I recently received a query from a Queen in central Florida regarding the "Southernese" usage of a word. She freely acknowledged that while technically she had for some years made her home in a Southern location—that didn't qualify her as Southern. I applauded her for knowing the difference. It's the whole kittens-in-the-oven-ain't-exactly-biscuits mistake that many Individuals Geographically Marooned Outside the South (IGMOS) often make. This Queen had the grace to at least know what she didn't know and so she came to the Font of All Wisdom—me, of course—for an explanation of the Southern usage of the word *ugly*.

She had encountered a group of women crowded together in a small area where many were vying for space and more were expected to arrive momentarily. One particular woman in the group kept remarking on how tight the quarters were and expressing her irritation at the anticipated advent of newcomers. Her complaining grew more intense, and as it did so, she began prefacing her venomous statements with the phrase "Now, I don't want to be ugly but . . ." Or she closed them with ". . . but I don't want to be ugly."

Queenie was nonplussed. WHO would WANT to BE UGLY? Why should it ever be necessary to state out loud for the benefit of others that one, in fact, did not harbor any secret hankerings to be deemed unattractive? Queenie was so distressed by the woman's continued disclaimer that she finally felt moved to speak up and assure the woman that she need have no fear, she was really quite fetching and in no danger whatsoever of being thought unfortunate-looking—not even plain—"You're really cute," she said with assurance.

And so Queenie was even more confused by the look she got in response to her kind offer of affirmation. "I couldn't tell if she thought I was stupid, rude, or out of my mind, but she clearly did not appreciate my attempt to bolster her confidence in her appearance."

"And then what happened?" I wanted to know. Queenie said she left to go to the bar after the woman blessed her heart and everybody else looked real uncomfortable.

Oh, my—poor Queenie. She had no idea what just happened to her. I explained to her that what the woman had been doing was venting her spleen about the poor planning that caused the overcrowded conditions and she was affixing the blame for her discomfort to a certain person or persons but she was not sufficiently displeased as to be willing to confront the planners face-to-face about the situation nor did she wish to be quoted on the matter, and thus, the all-purpose Southern anti-venom—"I don't want to be ugly, but . . ."

Ugly in this case is not describing an unattractive physical appearance—it means being unkind or unpleasant—and if one is Southern, one can freely SAY all the unkind, unpleasant—indeed, snipey and downright snarky—things one wants to say about another and then totally defuse it by assuring one's listeners that one "doesn't want to be ugly" about it.

About the heart blessing—I asked Queenie, "Did she laugh and give you a hug when she said it?" No, Queenie said—the woman gave her a pitying look, patted her hand, and said, "Bless your heart, hunny." "Was that bad?" she asked.

Oh, mercy—I knew instantly why the rest of the group had fallen into an uncomfortable silence. Queenie had just been dog-cussed by the quintessential Southern Woman—who still didn't want to be ugly.

This stuff cannot be taught, can it? Y'all all saw it coming from the first paragraph—and she STILL doesn't know what hit her. Bless her little heart.

Ahhh, my South—home of sweet tea, tall porches with ceiling fans, warm hospitality, and the most gracious hostility.

Asset-Preserving Tip

Stand in front of a good-quality mirror and practice smiling over-broadly while saying these words in as lilting a tone as you can muster: "Well, HEY, hun-ny! How ARE yew? You little steatopygious thing, yew! I swear, I do NOT know HOW yew do it! Yew are just A-MAZIN'! I don't think I could BEAR senectitude—but every time I see yew, I declare, yew just look like yew are eatin' it UP!"

The big smile and the sweet, bubbly tone are what will carry the day here on account of you have just told somebody that she looks as if she is thoroughly enjoying her immensely fat behind as well as her old age.

Buh-bye, now! Y'all come see us, y'hear?!

P.S.

While there may be the occasional misunderstanding about the use of the word *ugly* in reference to one's self and one's desire to not be so, there is, as far as I know, only ONE accepted use for the word *pretty*, and it means just that, which is not to say that no care need be taken in the use of it.

Case in point: A bunch of us Queens, all of or above a Certain Age, encountered a woman who, although admittedly younger than US, was still not likely to be considered exactly "YOUNG" by anybody's standards, and somehow or other this only-slightly-less-old-than-us woman worked it into the conversation that the great burden of her LIFE had always been that, in whatever crowd she found herself, SHE was always. . . . "The Pretty One." Oh, my, what an affliction.

Needless to say—as a group, we found this terribly off-putting, and the looks exchanged amongst us registered, wordlessly but nonetheless unanimously, the opinion that "either she must have always made sure to run with a fairly unattractive bunch of dog balls or she was perhaps giving herself unwarranted airs on account of, she was okay but we didn't think there was any overabundance of letters being written home about her great beauty."

Word to Those Wishing for Wisdom: While it is wonderful and certainly important to have and maintain a good opinion of one's appearance, it's generally best to let others notice it for themselves and offer any verbal confirmation they choose about the subject rather than introducing the topic one's self.

~16~

Help Is Close at Hand

There are times when Life Itsownself seems more difficult than it should be and we may feel the need for a bit of a leg up on a perplexing problem, and toward this end, we often seek the costly opinions of professional listeners.

I am of the opinion that—except in the case of true mental illness, which I believe is still fairly uncommon—most "therapy" amounts to expensive self-indulgence for those of us who have used up our free resources by wearing all available friends and family slap OUT with our never-ending whinings about our Situations, and now we would prefer to pay large sums of money to a stranger who is willing (for a price) to endlessly listen to our endless crap—as opposed to just, say, DOING something DIFFERENT.

What all GOOD "therapy" boils down to is this:

Patient: "It hurts when I do this."
Therapist: "Don't do that."

Now, you can pay thousands and thousands and a few more thousands of dollars over decades of your life to Talk About Your Problems—and that is certainly your prerogative—but sooner or later, if you want things to actually GET BETTER, there will come a Time when you identify what it is you're doing that's making you miserable and then, hopefully, shortly after that, there will come a time when you STOP doing whatever it is that's making you miserable and START doing something else instead. All I'm saying is—you could do that SOONER rather than LATER, if you was of a mind to, and that a therapist who is willing to "take you to raise" (for a fee) by endlessly indulging your fascination with yourself is not doing you any favors.

A GOOD therapist will help you identify your problem and your options for resolution—perhaps encourage you to choose one and act on it—and then send you on your way with some new tools for living your own life. You can pop back in the next time you need such help—it shouldn't be like a standing NAIL appointment, for crying out loud—which, now that you mention it, is kinda what it amounts to: crying out loud.

Endless Therapy—just like Worry—is not a substitute for taking action—it's something we do when we don't WANT to take action. And that's fine—as long as we know what we're doing—and not doing, as it were. But once more, let me say, I'm not talking about mental illness here—that requires an actual physician-type person and it is not within the personal power of the patient to control. Choosing to NOT use our personal power is infinitely different than not having any.

Okay, for all of us who just basically want to be rescued from whatever life situation we've gotten ourselves into—and who doesn't?—that would be SOOOO great if some mama or daddy figure could just pick us up and tell us don't worry about this for one second and then go fix it for us. Whooo-man—sign me up for THAT! However, that is NOT available, and even if it was, the line would be way too long—we'd prolly die before it was our turn. But, in lieu of actual rescue, perhaps some diversion would lighten your load.

Toward that end, let me suggest that you visit the Web site of Alexyss K. Tylor. She and her mama have a teevee show that airs on public access in the Atlanta area and they have got, as the evangelists love to say, a WORD for YOU today, my sistah! Ms. Tylor and her mama want us to know that we are GOD-DESSES and that we have, right there betwixt our very own legs, THE POWER—as in THE power—the MOST POWER-FUL power on THIS planet—that's right, VAGINA POWER trumps ALL.

And Ms. Tylor and her mama are here to tell us all how to put our very own Vagina Power to work not only for ourselves but for the whole world—especially for ourselves, though. My very favorite episode, so far, is where Ms. Tylor explains to her mama how it is that, on occasion, "DICK will make you SLAP SOMEBODY—inna FACE!"

I know I have found that to be true in my own life experience so many, many times—I just never fully understood WHY it happened—and now I do. You can have this understanding, too, and learn all the many ways that you have been underutilizing your Vagina Power, and, even better, the many more ways you can improve your interpersonal relationships, particularly with men, so that you need never again find yourself involved with a man to whom you have personally given Everything and from whom you have not even received so much as a shrimp dinner from Long John Silver's, which only costs, what? $2.49?

I'm telling you—Alexyss K. Tylor has some Answers for some of you this very day. The information is free—as is your choice to make good use of it. If you are consuming liquids when you access the show, make sure that you turn your head AWAY from your monitor and keyboard—the eruption from your nasal passages will destroy them.

I recently saw an ad in a small-town Southern newspaper for a man representing himself as a marriage counselor. It features a photo of him wearing a big smile and a rakish fedora hat, which inspired my confidence in him from the get-go. His lead-in was quite catchy, although somewhat cryptic, in my opinion:

"IT is what IT is," with the two *its* in all caps for emphasis. He claims the title of "Dr." and has the initials "B.Y.U." after his name, in parentheses. W.T.F.? Okay, and he's not JUST a doctor and a B.Y.U.—he's also a Prophet, excuse me, The Prophet AND The King of Wisdom.

Perhaps this is what has led to my rather less-than-high opinion of so many so-called therapists—none of the individuals from whom I personally ever sought help had the "B.Y.U." distinction and certainly none of them claimed overtly to be The Prophet and/or The King of Wisdom. Not a ONE of them EVER told me, "IT is what IT is." This explains a lot about me, in my opinion, and now that I KNOW that IT is what IT is, I expect things will be a lot different around here. And I got that for FREE, from his ad—I can only imagine how much more my life can be improved if I avail myself of his actual services for dollars.

In addition to marriage consulting—that's the next word he used in conjunction with marriage—is the consulting different from the counseling? I'll ask him and let you know—no charge. You can also get him to help you with Mental Dynamics—not sure what that is but it's bound to be good, don't you think? In addition, he can help you out with Spiritual Awareness—also sounds helpful—and then you can get some Brain Building.

My sister, Judy, wants to get some Brain Building assistance but I told her I thought it was a bad idea because unless she gets all her friends (and me) to sign up for it as well, she will not have anybody to talk to. She saw the wisdom of this theory right off.

The Good Doctor further states in his ad a description of What a Woman Needs—I read this part closely—being a woman and often in need, it was of particular interest to me. According to him, our needs are as follows:

- From ages 0 to 18 we need "Good Parents!" He uses an exclamation point so I will, too!
- From ages 18 to 35 we need "Good Looks!" That's all we need, or at least that's all he listed, but he also ended with an exclamation point so here you go!
- From ages 35 to 50 we need "Good Personality!"
- From ages 50 to 65 we need "CASH!"

There is no mention of any womanly needs that might arise from age 65 and older.

Well, he certainly has got it all figured out so I guess I'll be calling him, and I feel confident it will be the best money I ever spent—I can't wait for the New Me. I am happy that I am past the point of needing both good looks and good personality—whew, that's lucky!—and now am in the "cash only" phase of life. I am only hoping that he has some fund-raising ideas for ME that are as good as the one he's found for HIMSELF.

With any luck, I might even be able to open a branch office for him in Jackson. Need to know what the "B.Y.U." is—perhaps it's something I can already do—Blow You Up or Bring Your Underwear? Upon further inquiry, I learned that he offers counseling only on specific days—I would like that, setting my own hours and allowing for a lot of downtime—but he also offers a hand car-wash service, which I am under NO circumstances willing to do for anybody anytime. I won't even drive THROUGH a car wash. I'll be willing to work for less money and focus my energies solely on the counseling aspects with no bonus car washes thrown in. If you want the full-service deal, you'll just have to see him hisownself.

He closes his ad with yet another snappy but obscure motto: "REMEMBER, LET IT DO WHAT IT DO!" Uh-huh.

Now, SEE? And you thought life was so hard. If you're reading this as a youngster, great, I just saved you several decades of chasing your tail. If you're old, like me, well, it's better tardy than not at all, isn't it? Let's go lie down and ponder this great wisdom. I am SO READY to just let it do what it do.

Not sure what that means, though. Am I doing it now? Does this look right?

∽17∽

Living Will

My sister, Judy, and I have recently been lamenting the loss of our late and, we tell ourselves, very great minds. If you are over forty-six and a half years old, you know what we're talking about—at the moment anyway; in just a second, you'll forget what we're talking about.

Not only do we walk purposefully into rooms and forget the purpose for the trip, we even forget the WORDS to describe the purpose. The so-called experts assure us this is nothing to worry about. We don't trust them. We've seen them. They're old, too. They're just trying to convince THEMSELVES there's no problem here.

I'm telling you, it's a problem. Trying to write a book is hard enough if you have a decent vocabulary. The other day, I could NOT think of the word *nostalgia*. Ironic, huh? Also maddening. I called Judy, naturally; she has a most impressive command of the language, in my opinion. Of course, how hard is it to impress me? I can't think of fucking *nostalgia.*

I told her I was trying to think of a word that means remembering something fondly and she couldn't think of it either. We went back and forth, ending up practically hollering at each other in frustration over our mutual failure to come up with the word. She thought I was just being difficult and refusing to use any of the what she thought to be fine words that she offered. They were fine words indeed—they just didn't have any relation to the word *nostalgia.* Judy thought I was being nitpicky and stubborn in my refusal to settle for a different word, meaning nothwithstanding.

When *nostalgia* finally surfaced in my muddy brain, she insisted that she had offered me any number of words that meant the same exact thing and I said no she did not and she said yes she did, too, but then neither one of us could remember any of the words she'd suggested so that was the end of that.

She confessed that she had herself—just the other day—forgotten the word *croissant* and nearly lost her mind over it. Her housekeeper was going to the grocery store for her and Judy was wanting some . . . some . . . oh, shit, what are those things? It's hard to act out *croissant* even by the most creative actress for the most astute audience—neither of which was this duo. Judy finally got online and Googled "French pastries" and went down the list until she came to "croissant," and a great shout of jubilation could be heard throughout the Garden District of New Orleans.

A discussion ensued about what if we really were completely losing our minds and did I think she was and did she think I was and what would we do if either one of us really was and how could we tell and when would we know it was time to do something about it?

We both promised that whichever one of us was the last one still in possession of a brain cell would somehow kill the one who had lost all of hers. But how would we know when the Time had Come? This is a pretty important distinction and one we felt needed to be clearly defined for future reference.

It was therefore decided that it was okay that she could not remember the word *croissant*. She at least had the presence of mind to use Google to find it and, I might add, the great good sense to be sending someone else to the store to fetch it for her. However, the day she no longer knows what to DO with a croissant will be her last day. Likewise, she will know that if I start watching reality TV, quoting Dr. Phil, riding roller coasters, and seem to have forsaken bacon in favor of anything soy—it's time to Get the Pillow.

That's what—well, I can't tell you who but she's a nurse—says they all say when they've got a particularly cantankerous patient on their wing. They tell the night nurse, "It's time to get the pillow for 322," meaning "If you don't mind, and you have a minute, would you please smother that old bitch before I come back in the morning?" Nurses just have a wry sense of humor, don't they? I know a bunch of 'em who work for a place that has the words "continued care" in its title. They say it should actually read, "pretend to care." Which I find hilarious—as long as I'm not needing tending to, of course.

Asset-Preserving Tip

No matter WHAT your age—ALWAYS, ALWAYS, ALWAYS be very, very nice to nurses.

~18~

Our De-luxe Apartment Awaits

We, The Cutest Boy in the World and I, are making big check marks on each day of our calendar until November 23, 2012—for on THAT day, I will be sixty and therefore qualified to move into the retirement home where my mama lives—The Waterford, or, as we like to think of it, Old Folks' Heaven. You have to be at least sixty to live there, and at that low age, I think you also have to have some sort of infirmity, but I don't think that will be too hard for me to come up with, so we're counting on it.

Kyle, of course, can go only on MY coattails since HE will be only a mere whippersnapperish fifty then, fie on his young ass. Don't you know he will be some kind of popular up in there? I mean, the most wiveled up, decrepit ole boy in the joint can have all the old women he could ever want in those places, and actually, if they survive that long, they're prolly a pretty good bet, so maybe it's no wonder they are in such hot demand with the ladies. But KYLE, at fifty, will be like anybody else's thirty—I'll have to guard my meds to make sure them old biddies don't try to poison me to get at him.

We have been dying to move in ever since Mama moved there a few years back. For next to nothing a month, she gets three meals a day—restaurant-style, although they will bring it to you in your room if you are feeling particularly slack-assy at a given mealtime—housekeeping, laundry service, all her utilities, including cable, except for her telephone, and they will drive her anywhere she wants or needs to go. They all go to the casinos once a month, Wal-Mart once a week. She has a kitchen, should she develop an inexplicable desire to cook something for herownself—this has not happened so far, but it's nice to have the option, just in case. She can have pets and/or overnight company if she gets a hankering for either. And, of course, there's BINGO. Several times a week, there's bingo. Mostly they play for paper products—toilet paper and paper towels, which I find hilarious—but once a week it's DIME BINGO and they play for cash. It is possible to win as much as four dollars at one of these tension-packed games.

And you better believe they are tension-packed, too. Even for the toilet paper games, you'll see the seasoned pros enter the game-room closet at least two hours before the first number is due to be called—to root through the box of bingo cards and select the "best" ones for themselves. All the cards have markings on the back put there—and understood—by the various hard-core players. Venturing near that closet before bingo time is not unlike wading off into piranha-packed waters with corn dogs strapped to your ankles. These are the women who, only a couple of decades back, could be seen snatching up Cabbage Patch dolls at pre-Christmas sales with woe, woe, woe, and multiple wounds and lacerations to anybody who thought about interfering with their snatching. These women will tear your arm off and club you with it for the right bingo card—they have not exactly mellowed with age.

That would be just SUCH an understatement. I think the myth of sweet old people is kinda like the whole jolly fat people thing—an occasional coincidence but certainly not a given. Testimony: A friend of mine's mother-in-law had recently moved into a similar retirement home and, in an effort to help her win friends and influence people in the home, Good Daughter-in-law volunteered to bring goodies for the home-wide Valentine's party. Unfortunately, one of the residents chose that very day to shoot himself in the head, thereby threatening to dampen the whole celebration, death by self-inflicted gunshot wounds being a widely acknowledged party buzzkill, retirement home or not.

Good D-I-L half-expected to be notified by the staff of the party's cancellation, but to the contrary, the general consensus was that it was important to go on living, even though one of their members had so recently chosen to stop. So, off to the home she goes with all her cute pink, heart-shaped tasties, and just as she's getting it all set up and the crowd is gathering, here the funeral-home folks come through the lobby, pushing a sheet-covered gurney, followed closely by the assorted recently bereaved who had come to do whatever must be done in these cases.

Without bothering to lower their voices in the slightest, perhaps assuming that the next of kin were all as deaf as they were, they began a lively discussion about the suicidee. "Well, I knew he was depressed but I never thought he'd shoot himself."

Good D-I-L is trying to climb over furniture to get to them to silence them, at least until after the guy's body is out the door. Not much luck.

"Me neither, I thought he'd take pills." "Well, I thought he might slash his wrists." "Naw, I always thought he'd hang himself." "HANG himself—there's no place to hang yourself in here. What do you mean, hang himself?" "Well, I don't know—from the doorknob maybe?" "DOORKNOB—well, that's just STUPID, you can't HANG yourself from a DOORKNOB—that's how you PULL a TOOTH, you idiot!"

My friend Tammy's mom was also trying out life in a retirement home but she was not taking to it with any particular enthusiasm. The one upside of it, as far as she was concerned, was that she only had to go down the hall to the card room to play bridge two or three times a week. Regular easy access to bridge that did not require hosting the game in her own quarters was a definite plus in her estimation.

Tammy came by to check on Mom one afternoon. She would frequently time her visits to fall just a few minutes before bridge time because Mom would NOT be late and risk losing her favorite spot at her favorite table to some swifter septuagenarian and thus any whining time was severely curtailed. So when Tammy popped into Mom's room at 2:38 PM one Wednesday for a few minutes of prebridge chatting, she was dismayed to find Mom sitting in the semidark, in her robe and in an absolutely foul humor.

As much as she hated to utter the words, she really had no choice but to ask, "What's wrong?" and brace herself for the whine-fest she strongly suspected she was in for. "Oh, it's just been a TERRIBLE day—ole Bob Smith tried to slash his wrists right after lunch." Naturally, Tammy was aghast at this news, and, at the same time, somewhat chagrined at her own selfish thoughts of early escape that she had admittedly indulged in as she approached her mother's room only moments before.

"OMIGOD, that is AWFUL!" Tammy cried. "Is he . . . did he . . . how is he?" "Oh, he's gonna be FINE, he barely bled at ALL, and they made such a BIG FUSS over it and hauled him off to the nuthouse—and NOW WE DON'T HAVE A

FOURTH! This is just like him, selfish, selfish, selfish—if he wasn't gonna do any more damage than THAT, he coulda at least waited till after we played bridge. Men, I swear."

If this is how they react to suicide, successful and otherwise, in their own ranks, it should give you some idea of how little value they will place on your life and assorted limbs when it comes to getting the good bingo cards. Consider yourself forewarned.

So moving in when I am only sixty will have yet another advantage—I haven't seen an old woman over there yet that I don't think I can take, but having a few years' youth on them sure won't hurt. And of course, if they give me much trouble, I can use Kyle—either for distraction or, should the pushing come to shoving, muscle.

I'm quite fond of bingo myself. Well, actually, what I really like is hollering "BINGO!" I may have mentioned that before—I think hollering "BINGO" in a crowded room is a highly underrated joy and there just aren't enough regular opportunities in everyday life to do it. I mean, I suppose one could just haul off and holler it anytime one wanted to, no law against it that I ever heard. I mean, it's not like yelling "FIRE" or "RUN FOR YOUR LIVES" or anything, but really, unless there is competition and some kind—any kind—of prize waiting to be won, well, it just loses something—for me anyhow.

At Christmas, somebody's handbell choir can be counted on to make an appearance at the home. For some reason, handbell choirs have always pissed me off in an almost Holden Caulfield "good luck" kind of way. I mean, it's not exactly one of your more marketable skills for an individual. I mean, it's not like SINGING in a choir, where you have to know the whole tune and all the words and you COULD sing those whole songs for anybody, anytime. If you're a handbeller, all you come away with is the knowledge of your particular "ding-dings" at the appointed time in the various songs, which doesn't strike me as the kind of thing that's likely to come in handy at some point down the road.

If one was a singer, one could sing songs to oneself to pass the time if one was, for whatever reason, in solitary confinement, and not drive everybody crazy making some kind of repetitive racket, like Steve McQueen in *The Great Escape* with his baseball. You would not want to be anywhere near a handbeller in solitary confinement—you'd go crazy listening to the random dings, not being able to hear the rest of the song and all.

I saw a FABULOUS xylophone player (now, there's an oxymoron for you) in some "scholarship" pageant. Of course, she wasn't REALLY a xylophone player—she was a former HAND-BELLER with a xylophone and an audio track instead of a bunch of other handbellers. She had learned to play HER notes, with much flair and enthusiasm, at the appropriate times during the song—the rest of the time, she occupied herself with grinning real big, slinging her big hair around, and cleaving for the judges. The great thing that happened was the tape stopped working after the first couple of bars—so you could actually TELL that she was playing only about twenty-seven or so notes in the whole song. But did she let a little equipment malfunction stop HER quest for the crown? HA! In a pig's eye—whatever THAT means—she just FOCUSED ALL her concentration on hearing that song in her head. You could tell she was focused because she stopped grinning and rather gripped her tongue between her lips and almost frowned a teeny bit as she clearly counted off the beats in her head, and you could tell she was counting because she was bobbing her head rhythmically—until it was TIME and then she grinned REAL BIG and very elaborately performed her little "deedle-eedle-eet"—then resumed focused counting until the next "deedle-eedle-eet" opportunity came up in the song.

It was a stellar moment in the harum-scarum world of Women's Scholarships.

Okay, here's one concern I have about moving into a retirement home: the overall color scheme and decor in the public areas. What is up with mauve anyway? Who can we hold responsible for the proliferation of this wretched noncolor? It is just EVERY damnwhere, I swear, but it is slathered all over retirement homes. Every surface in the common areas of The Waterford is either mauve or forest green. Are those the official colors of the Greatest Generation or something? If so, then maybe by the time I move in, they will no longer be the major demographic in the home and the color scheme will be changed to whatever the official Baby Boomer colors are, and I have no idea what those might be but it's got to be an improvement over the mauve/green thing.

While I'm complaining about the flaws in my future residence, in addition to the mind-numbing color scheme, there are also way too many prints of puppies and blond children hanging in the halls, in the parlors, in the library, in the club room. The only place they don't have one is in the entrance vestibule—that's where they have the NO FIREARMS ALLOWED sign, which always tickles me for some reason.

But anyway, with the notable exception of the unfortunate decor and the possibility of being subjected to the occasional handbell choir, these retirement homes seem really swell to me. You have all the comforts of home with the service and lack of responsibility of a hotel. What is not to love? You have to go outside to smoke, of course, and that's somewhat inconvenient, although it shouldn't really come up for me personally until I reach the age of eighty if, in fact, I make it that long. If I do somehow manage to live that long, I definitely plan to resume smoking, but perhaps by then they will have decided once again that smoking IS good for you and I'll be encouraged by my physician to smoke at least a pack a day and my Medicare will pay for it.

Truly, the only reason my (asthmatic) mama ever smoked in her life was because her DOCTOR TOLD HER TO—for weight loss. I think it was the first near-death pneumonia experience that planted that little doubt seed in her mind and caused her to quit—against the best medical advice available at the time.

But surely you've noticed that deadly stuff seems to come and go in cycles? About every five or ten years, everything we enjoy becomes poisonous and sure to cause death at any moment, and then in a few years, seems like they decide, nah, it's actually good for you. I can remember in the eighties there was much ranting, on a national level and by assorted local health professionals to me personally, about the dangers and evils of chocolate. I told them all, to a man, "I am SORRY if chocolate is bad for YOU—but I can ASSURE you, it is VERY, VERY GOOD for ME," and I just went right on munching away. And it's a good thing I did since NOW they all say you'll die tomorrow if you DON'T eat a pound or so of chocolate as fast as you can.

So, I figure by the time I'm eighty, cigarettes will be back in good graces. Can't happen soon enough for me. I did LOVE to smoke. Hated how it made me feel—and we won't even discuss the stench—but, man, wasn't it fun to DO? November 23, 2032—I'll be the one out in back of The Waterford in the birthday hat—smoking.

Hope for the Nest That Just Won't Empty

As I think about it, I believe it would be positively BRILLIANT to offer this kind of living arrangement for all Parents of What

OUGHT to Be FULLY GROWED Children Who Refuse to Move Out and Become Adults. I mean, if you find yourself currently in possession of a thirty-year-old live-in KID, what WOULDN'T you be willing to PAY to have a "home" to send him/her to—just to get him/her out of your HOUSE? It is an idea whose time has apparently long since come, if my friends and neighbors are any indication of a trend, and I believe they are. One girl I know has a son who's got to be pushing thirty-five who is piled up in his childhood room, looking at porn on the Internet and whining about mealtimes and gas money, having big parties at her house when she goes out of town, and leaving trash, dirty laundry, and empty liquor cabinets wherever he goes. I guess it's too late to beat him, but it sure would be gratifying, I'm thinking. She would, I feel certain, be willing to pay THOUSANDS of dollars every month to move him to a nice place where he could be somebody else's problem.

Then, at least, she could one day die in peace, knowing that her little baby would be well cared for in her absence and he could just dwell in fairyland forever. What a comfort that would be to so many parents whose baby birds have staunchly resisted flying lessons. And this concept would also make for some excellent employment opportunities for aging Boomers—since we created these lazy-ass monsters, who better to hire to serve them? I mean, we already know how they like their eggs and all.

Asset-Preserving Tip

For parents of very young children—try to identify some older parents in your community who appear to have done a good job of raising their own children to be well adjusted, independent adults. Then leave your own children on their doorstep and run away.

For parents of adult-aged infants—see if you can get into the Witness Protection Program.

For childless adults—continue having fun!

~19~

Everything Old Is Cute Again

I am so looking forward to being Born Again Cute. It takes awhile, evidently, but I am seeing it happen all around me more and more every day—I figger sooner or later, it's got to get around to me as well. Once you pass a certain age, and I'm not totally sure of what the magic number is yet, I'll keep you posted—but after that age, anything you do is considered just the cutest thing they ever heard by everybody who hears about it.

How liberating is that? You can say and do anything that you take a mind to and everybody will laugh fit to kill over it—stuff that would have gotten you shunned, banned, and/or arrested just a few short years before now serves only to further endear you to the world at large.

Seven or eight years ago, a bunch of us went on Delbert

McClinton's Sandy Beaches Cruise—yes, there really is a Delbert cruise, and yes, it really is unbelievably fun and fabulous in every way. Go to www.delbert.com and sign yourself up—tell 'em I sent you. Anyway, besides having one of those true time-of-your-life experiences, we also got a really swell souvenir that we kept and treasure to this very day—Ellyn and Frances. Frances is the mom of Ellyn—also the boss of—but, then, Frances is the boss of EVERYBODY, so that's not unusual. Frances is also the mom of one of my favorite singer/songwriters of all time, Jesse Winchester. You would know him from "Mississippi You're On My Mind," "Twigs and Seeds," and "Rhumba Man," but you oughta know him for a whole lot more—trust me on this and give him a listen.

All that is to say that Ellyn and Frances are natural-born music lovers. Now, Frances is also a lover of cruises and she had been nagging Ellyn for quite some time to take her on a trip. Ellyn, devoted daughter though she may be, was not overly thrilled at the prospect of spending a week at sea with her mom, as you might possibly be able to imagine. And then she chanced upon the Delbert cruise. Without even checking with Frances, Ellyn booked them both to sail with Delbert and Friends and then called and said, "Mama, pack your bags, I'm taking you on that cruise you've been wanting!"

If you've ever been on a cruise, you know that sometimes they assign tablemates for meals. Well, there were six in our party—three couples—and when we arrived at dinner that first night at sea, we were presented with Ellyn and Frances. Talk about your love at first sight. Ellyn, of course, was thrilled to make our acquaintance as well, but that was mostly because she immediately saw in us six able-bodied individuals who could be pressed into service—the service of Frances, naturally, and she do require a whole heap of servicing, Mizz Frances do.

I don't even know how old she was then, but suffice it to say we were pretty sure she was older than any of us, though you'd never know it by the schedule she kept, the dance partners she wore out, and/or the musicians who fell in love with her. I don't think Nick Connolly will ever get over Frances but he's hardly alone in that distinction.

Frances was at every performance of every musician for the EN-tire week, which also meant that Ellyn was in attendance as well, except for the times when she (Frances) had a date with Bruce Browning. Now, Bruce was actually on the cruise with TammyCarol, but occasionally TammyCarol would do boring stuff, like sleep, which left Bruce at loose ends, which is never a good situation to leave your musician boyfriend in for very long, so before retiring for the night, TammyCarol would hand Bruce off to Frances. I still think that was pretty trusting of TammyCarol, but perhaps it was more a case of extreme exhaustion taking precedence over the possibility of losing one's boyfriend permanently to an older but livelier woman. TammyCarol decided the calculated risk was worth just about anything to get a few uninterrupted z's.

Frances does love a good story—she particularly loves to

TELL a good story or twenty. The woman can flat talk, now, I am telling you. Luckily for us all, she is hilarious. On the occasion that Ellyn might dare to chime in and begin to tell a tale of her own, Frances would listen for a time—a very short time usually—and then, Mama-like, she would shush Ellyn and tell her to please "be quiet and let somebody else talk for a change," meaning, of course, HER. We found this endlessly entertaining—all of us but Ellyn, I guess.

The cruise, like all good things, did come to an end, but the love affair that was born on the high seas (they were higher for some than for others, I suspect) among the six of us and this delightful Mother-Daughter duo has lived on and on. Ellyn is now an O-fficial SPQ-in-Training, which means she has not yet been formally initiated (by making her public Promise to the High Muckety-Muck at the newspaper), but she does get to ride on the float in the Million Queen March the third weekend of every March in Jackson, Mississippi. She also gets to leave her home in Pendleton, Oregon—which is FAR away, no matter where you are—and come to Jackson a week or so BEFORE the Parade and basically be my bitch on float-building detail. She counts herself lucky in this—which is one of her more endearing qualities.

For several years on her trek from Oregon to Mississippi, Ellyn would swing by Memphis and pick up Frances so that she could ride in the Parade with the Queen Mothers and Used-to-Be's. Of course, of all the QMs, Frances was the only one who danced all Friday night at the SPQ™ Ball.

Then, in 2005, Frances moved to a retirement home in Memphis and got herself a new boyfriend. She did not come to the Parade that year because she was too afraid to go off and leave Tommy unattended—she did not trust them ole biddies to keep their mitts off her Tommy, and apparently, there was also not much faith that Tommy would resist any mitts that came his way.

Last year, I was the Honorary Chair for the Susan G. Komen Race for the Cure® in Little Rock, Arkansas—which is, last time I checked, the third largest Komen race in the country. They have more than forty-three thousand runners—and they allow only women to run. The men pay their entry fees to line up on either side of the course and form the Three Miles of Men—in support of the women running—don't you love that? A number of the Queens went with me from Jackson and Ellyn flew down from Oregon. Of course, she went by and got Frances, too.

We were putting on our "travel outfits" to wear to the big party on Friday night before the race. Frances was sitting in our suite, watching all the preparations and primping. Ellyn, wearing a very short sequined and feathered skirt, black fishnets, and assorted other trashy accessories, came and stood quietly by Frances's chair as Frances was holding forth to anybody within earshot about various and sundry subjects of interest to herownself. Out of the corner of her eye, she noticed that someone was standing next to her chair. Glancing up—but apparently not all the way up—she said, "Oh, my, don't you look darlin'! Look at your cute outfit—why, you could just go out on the town anywhere in that and be the cutest one there!" And then about the time she reached the end of that sentence, she did look all the way up and realized it was, in fact, her own daughter, Ellyn, standing there in that outfit, and without taking another breath, she barked, "MY GOD, YOU LOOK LIKE HELL! I HOPE YOU DON'T THINK YOU'RE GOING OUT—WITH ME—WEARING THAT THING!"

We were all falling down with assorted beverages spewing from our nostrils, helplessly howling at the Two Faces of Frances and the one priceless face on Ellyn as the full fury of Frances the Indignant fell upon her. Really, it was impossible for us to decide which was funnier but we thoroughly enjoyed it all.

Then, as we traveled en masse down the hall toward the elevators—I was to be the Duck Master that evening for the Famous Peabody Ducks (if you don't know what that is, bless your heart—Google "the Peabody" to find out) and I did not want to be late. Those ducks have a schedule to keep, after all. Anyway, Frances was grumbling and mumbling and muttering under her breath in Ellyn's general direction all the way down the hall. As we boarded the elevator, Frances said, to no one in particular, "Hmmph, well, I just believe if I had known that I was gon' be wearin' that, I believe I woulda lost some weight." We nearly tee-teed in the Peabody elevator. If we had, we would have totally blamed it on those ducks.

Alas, and now we learn that our beloved party-girl Frances

has Alzheimer's, just ever so slightly, and so she's moved to an Alzheimer's care facility in Pendleton, to be near her devoted daughter, Ellyn. She knows everybody in the world, except, of course, for her main caregiver, Ellyn, and Ellyn's husband, Tom. Frances calls him "That Man," so she at least remembers his face, just not his name. Ellyn's identity and the reasons for her repeated visits are a mystery, but still welcome ones, at least.

We mourn the loss of Frances, as we knew and loved her, but we rejoice at the very strong evidence that she is, in fact, still in there, somewhere. We know this because Frances has yet another boyfriend. Not sure what his name actually is, but she calls him Tommy because she recalls being fond of someone by that name. He seems happy to be Tommy, whether he is or not. New Tommy has a wife—on the Outside—who was somewhat perplexed as to what her appropriate response should be to the budding romance between her husband and Ellyn's mother. Frances has no idea that she is carrying on with a married man. She's been told but she forgets, which is handy because she is quite taken with her new Tommy.

Tommy still sometimes knows that he does, in fact, still have a wife and he often recognizes her when she comes to visit. However, as he tells everyone, SHE no longer likes to kiss him—and Frances DOES—so, duh, Frances wins. Ellyn convinced the wife to get over it and be happy that the two lovebirds have found each other since neither possesses the ability to consciously do anything wrong.

Only Frances could find a way to turn Alzheimer's into a Romantic Getaway. Even in death, she will BE the Life of the Party. That's our Frances, God love her.

Asset-Preserving Tip

If we would all just try to be a LITTLE BIT like Frances—every day—not only our own lives, but the whole wide world, would be a better place.

20

Love Among the Ruins

I wish I could tell you that once you get past the initial shock and awe of puberty and the emotional holocaust of adolescence—you survive all that and pass into young adulthood—you find that, well, stuff still seems pretty much every bit as dramatic and traumatic as it did in junior high school but you slog on, thinking perhaps cruising altitude is just on the other side of maybe just a couple more bumpy layers—and you emerge, bloodied but unbowed, well, maybe a little bowed but still mostly on your feet, to find yourself in full-blown middle age and you think, well, okay fine, NOW—things are gonna get easier—just like in that old song, you know, "Whoo-ooh, chi-i-ild, things are gonna get easier"—I WISH I could tell you that is what's waiting round the bend, my huckleberry friend, but guess what—whoo-oooh—chi-i-ild—it ain't. Things are gonna get more the same.

I know it's not the news you wanted to hear—I wish I had something better to report from over here in Geezerville. I mean, you WOULD THINK that, sooner or later, we would sorta have all our Life Lessons more or less down and could just coast for our downhill slides, but no. Not only are we ON the downhill slide but it's not even a smooth slide—it's full of splinters and a bunch of big rocks and there's hardly any water to ease our way. Yes, it's not so much like whooshing with smooth, slick speed down a playground slide as it is like being shoved down the side of a very craggy mountain.

I had my own set of false assumptions about the naturally easy self-reliance and competency that would be mine just by virtue of reaching adulthood and nobody I can recall ever contradicted any of them or offered any evidence to the contrary, so all this came as an utter shock to me, and perhaps you will fare better for at least having the benefit of this warning. I also assumed that relationships would somehow magically become uncomplicated and simple and that dating would be easier and more fun.

When none of that manifested itself in my own personal life, I thought for a time that perhaps it was just me. Perhaps everybody else in the world was in a comfy sail through life, with all the work and money issues long since resolved; they were just laid-back, having rational, intelligent, drama-free relationships with their friends and lovers, and that it was somehow just me and my chosen ones that were wallowing in a mire that seemed more than vaguely reminiscent of all the ones we'd wallowed in since the seventh grade.

It made me feel a bit better—and perhaps it will help you as well—to learn that nothing really ever gets better for anybody. Ever. So, even though there is NO HOPE—at least there is parity. We take our comfort where we can, I suppose.

Queen Susan—of one of the Georgia branches of the Turnip Green Queens—assures me that dating after fifty is every bit as much fun as watching golf on TV while sitting on an ant bed in the sun, drinking warm, curdly milk. So, if there's no golf on and you're fresh out of sour milk and ant beds on a cloudy day—just go ahead on that date from Matchmewithaperfectnightmare.com—you'll hardly notice the difference.

Now, I do know of a few people who've had some swell dates from those online services—even know a few who married folks they met that way—but whoo, boy, you talk about a slim minority. Most of the folks I talk to are like my friend Shar, who met a guy who was a for-real plumber online. Now, in my opinion, a plumber ranks way up on the Desirability Scale—I'd put him below a plastic surgeon (naturally, at my age, in my condition) but well above an attorney (I rarely break any significant laws) and certainly higher than a stockbroker (too suicidal). An able-bodied, WORKING plumber—CAN YOU EVEN IMAGINE THE LUXURY of having your own PER-

SONAL plumber? Well, that's a fantasy for us all, isn't it? So Shar was pretty tickled to find him and naturally felt a twinge of "he could be The One" from their first conversation.

For their first date, he took her to an extremely nice restaurant and she was greatly encouraged by the fact that he was willing and able to pay for this excursion and that he also seemed well acquainted with silverware and acceptable tableside behavior.

Then "Ralph" invited her to a home-cooked meal at his place for their second date and they spoke on the phone many times during the week, planning the entire menu, start to finish. And so, imagine Shar's surprise when she arrived at Chez Ralph at the appointed time and it was apparent that there had been no preparation for the much-discussed dinner—whatsoever. Ralph's mind was clearly Elsewhere—and WHERE was the evening's Big Surprise.

Ralph's house was not far from a local carnival-type establishment that featured games of all kinds, and the oh-so-lucky winners of all those games would take home PRIZES, the likes of which I don't believe are available for mere purchase anywhere in the world. If you can't win it, you just can't have it. But the more Shar looked around, as she was listening to the explanation for the no-dinner situation she currently found herself in, the more she realized she had found herself a real Winner— in the LOSER department.

Ralph's entire abode was decorated in carnival crap—

Tweety-Bird throws, Harley-Davidson memorabilia, Elvis throw pillows, stuffed EVERYTHING, fiber-optic angels. NASCAR was well represented, as were all the major breweries—Shar was certain there was a thousand-gallon tank of goldfish some-where—any prize you've ever seen at any carnival ever was in his house, in spades.

The REASON why Ralph had been unable to perform—in the kitchen—was that he had been completely distracted by a phone call he'd received shortly before Shar arrived. It seems that the carnival operator guy had CALLED him—personally, on the telephone—Ralph was on a first-name, exchanged-phone-numbers basis with the CARNY MAN—and alerted him to the fact that the carnival had just received a new ship-ment of LAVA LAMPS—and included in that shipment was at least one PURPLE one—and he knew that Ralph had not yet won a PURPLE lava lamp.

Okay, so far we've got no dinner, a house full of hideous cheap crap, and a guy (albeit a plumber) who is on the speed-dial of the carny man—who KNOWS what color lava lamps the guy has NOT YET won and furthermore knows that the man will NOT REST until he has won them in all colors currently available on planet Earth. And we have Shar—receiving all this most unwelcome information and it is truly disheartening—nearly disemboweling—and then Ralph asks her would she mind forgoing dinner for a frozen burrito so they could get on down to the carnival place—as he opened a desk drawer and took out a three-inch-thick roll of tickets, indicating that he had only about HALF of what he would NEED in order to win that PURPLE lava lamp—but he oughta be done in about four hours, give or take.

The neighbors still marvel at the length of the tire marks she left on the street that evening as she peeled off in her escape.

I'm sure you are joining me in asking that most troublesome yet universal question: WHERE DO THESE GUYS COME FROM? I'm sure I don't know—and neither does Shar— but she guesses that the Pez-collecting attorney she went out with next is from the same place. Picture it, a Pez house— towels, sheets, pillowcases, throw rugs—everything that could carry the Pez image was doing so—PLUS, shelf after shelf, in every single room, with thousands and thousands of PEZ dispensers—a-a-a-l-l-l lined up, nice and neat. Millions of little Pezzy eyes, just looking at you—a-a-a-l-l-l the time.

Shar needs new tires now.

How to Get More If You're a Guy

Okay, in all seven of my previous writings, I have either directly or indirectly schooled you guys on this subject. My own personal precious husband, The Cutest Boy in the World, is constantly exhorting men to read my books, touting them as

"Manuals on How to Get Laid," due to the high volume of content addressing the manifold sins of the male population that lead to their being Denied or Cut Off from Opportunities of a Carnal Nature with us, the Sinned Against.

But this is one subject I have never before even touched on and so y'all need to PAY REAL GOOD ATTENTION, OKAY? This is every bit as important as The Six Magic Words that I gave you in *God Save the Sweet Potato Queens*—remember them? Six TINY little words that, when said together and with sincerity, are guaranteed to melt the heart of any living woman. Just in case you forgot, here they are—one more time—"OH, NO—let ME handle THAT!"

Okay, so this information I am about to share with you has been gleaned from countless girl-type discussions over an even higher number of cocktails and it is 100 percent reliable. More than one woman has, in fact, BEGGED me to disseminate this fact in hopes that their guys will be educated by it.

This information is intended for those men who are in long-term relationships with a woman they still adore and who seems to still feel reciprocal adoration but who, for some reason, is no longer quite as forthcoming with the Goods as she once so eagerly was.

It's still happening—and when it does, it's still swell and all—but the spontaneity, the spark, the gotta-have-it-NOW seems to have wandered off. Here's where it went:

It went to wherever THE KISSING went. Every sex article

you read goes on and on about the importance of foreplay and blah blah blah—but what MEN fail to understand—and what we have so far been incapable of COMMUNICATING to them—is that BEFORE the FORE-play commences, there needs to be a substantial amount of KISSING.

Every woman I know, regardless of age, who is in a relationship that has lasted long enough for the jets to have cooled down a bit, says that she is happy with her partner. They're glad they are no longer "looking," but they ALL miss "making out." Their faces all become wistful at its mere mention. "O-O-O-O-OHHH . . ." they sigh, and you can tell the memories are fond, if not fresh.

Ever wonder why women will watch the movie *Bull Durham* every single time it airs on any network, at any time of the day or night? Google Kevin Costner's "I believe in" speech from that movie and pay particular attention to the line regarding long, slow, deep, soft, wet kisses that last three days. And then note, with interest, Susan Sarandon's response. Her eyes are glazed over, her jaw has dropped, and all she can say is a very breathless "Oh, my."

Oh, my, indeed. This is what is known as a Word to the Wise—and it SHOULD be, as they say, Sufficient.

You're welcome.

~21~

Eat What You Like and Die Like a Man

You should know: The food in all my books, this one included, IS POISON. IF you eat it all the time, you WILL die and you will die with a HUGE ass; however, that being said, it is, in my opinion, excellent for your disposition, which does count for a lot in this life. And so, here are a few more menu items to cheer you along on those days when you just feel the need for a Little Something—or a Lot. Some are more poisonous than others, but I believe that they all meet at least our minimal standards for delectable toxicity.

Queen of the Night Salsa 2.0

This is a jazzed-up version of an earlier recipe from our Precious Darlin' George. He is ever seeking new and more delicious ways to please us and we adore him for this and other reasons.

. . .

MIX ALL THIS stuff together—1 15-ounce can drained and rinsed black beans, 1 11-ounce can Niblets corn, 1 small can chopped green chilis, 1 small can chopped black olives, 2 to 3 chopped fresh tomatoes, at least 8 ounces shredded Monterey Jack, 1 bunch chopped green onions, some cilantro (fresh or dried, to taste), ½ teaspoon chili powder, ½ teaspoon cumin, ½ to ¾ of a 16-ounce bottle of Wishbone Robusto Italian dressing, and a whole big lot of chopped-up bacon. Obviously, the more bacon, the better—duh.

Chill all that overnight in the refrigerator and then eat it all at one sitting the next day with Fritos.

Don't Ask Me Again for the Pineapple Vodka Recipe

This recipe has circulated around the Queendom for a year or so now, and for some reason, nobody can ever hold on to it, and so when they get to craving it, e-mails fly about the country wildly until somebody can find it again. SO HERE IT IS—put this book in a safe place. You'll prolly be thirsty after eating all those Fritos with the Queen of the Night Salsa 2.0—so make this in advance—you'll be sooo glad you did.

. . .

GET 8 OR 10 (20-ounce) cans of pineapple rings packed in JUICE—do NOT get the kind packed in syrup. Drain the juice off as much as you can—you don't have to, like, blot the pineapple or anything—don't try to complicate this—it's easy. Dump the drained pineapple into a great big container and pour a liter of GOOD vodka over it. Put the lid on the jar or bowl and put it in the refrigerator and let it sit there—LET IT SIT THERE— for one week. One week is 7 days—so after 7 days have come and gone—then you may drain off your vodka and get reeeally happy. Just shake it with ice and pour it into your chilled martini glass and mmmmmm.

Don't obsess over the size of the cans or anything else. Just as long as you get a whole lot of pineapple in the vodka and let it sit and soak, it'll be fine. This is not one of your real technical recipes—it really is as simple as it sounds—so just do it.

Some people freeze the pineapple rings and then put them in Sierra Mist—which sounds delightful to me. Some people figger the pineapple has done its job and they just throw it away. I'm thinking a vodka-soaked pineapple ring is a handy thing to have in the freezer—bound to come in handy.

Sweet Scott's Great Nasty Recipe

Scott Caples is one of our newest Spud Studs and we do love him a LOT. He comes to every one of my book signings within two hundred miles of him and he brings divine deviled eggs and all manner of other tasty morsels—to soothe me in my travels. He is also really cute, a very snappy dresser with impeccable manners, and he comes to the Parade now—so y'all can meet him when you come to Jackson—one more reason why you need to come.

Scott sent me this SHOCKINGLY trashy recipe and it's just so good, I knew y'all would love it, too. This is one of those that is just SO BAD—you'll prolly want to lie and say you would never make such a thing. That's what I do—and that way I don't have to share it with anybody.

.   .   .

BROWN A POUND of ground beef—maybe drain off some of the grease if it's, like, swimming—totally your call—and then add 2 tablespoons minced onion and cook it for a minute. In a Pam'd casserole dish, combine half the meat with a can of cream of chicken soup, then add the rest of the meat and top that with a can of Cheddar cheese soup. Cover all that wondrous glop with 2 cups of shredded VELVEETA, and on top of THAT put 20 or so TATER TOTS, and bake it all at 350°F for about an hour.

Is that disgusting or WHAT? You will feel so guilty eating it,

I know, but hey, life is short. Actually, it will be a whole lot shorter if you eat this crap very often—but every once in a while, I think we deserve to eat something really revolting yet yummy.

Health-Nut Family's Famous Fried Apples

Queen Susie, who sent me this recipe, seems to me to be clearly a full-fledged tree-hugging, patchouli-wearing health-food fanatic. Here's the way she concocts a typical meal: she slices Jonathan apples very thin—without even peeling them first—and she cuts a whole lot of hickory-smoked bacon into little bitty bits. Then she fries the bacon bits until they're almost done, and at that point she dumps in all the unpeeled apple slices and puts a lid on the skillet for a little while.

When the apples are cooked almost clear, she dumps in a "cloud" of white sugar. (I'm thinking dark brown might be even better, what do you think?) She stirs that around a little and covers it again and cooks it until the apples start to look like candy.

Then she says—and I quote, "Serve as a meal with warm bread—we use whole wheat or multigrain because we watch our health." I love her.

Little Larva's Homicidal Maniac and Cheese

That cute little baby girl Alexis sent me this recipe with the caveat that it is a double-sided funeral food: eat enough of it at a funeral and the next funeral can be your own. Worth it, though.

• • •

COOK A COUPLE of pounds of macaroni and just hang on—we'll get back to it in a minute. Fry a whole lot of thick-sliced bacon—you'll need at least a half dozen slices for this recipe, so however much more than that you need to fry in order to end up with 6 slices after you've stuffed yourself—cook that much.

Then melt ½ stick butter and 2 cups Gruyère cheese in 1½ cups milk. Now dump your cooked macaroni into your Crock-Pot®—ooooh, I love my Crock-Pot®—and pour in a can of Cheddar cheese soup, 3 cups grated extra-sharp Cheddar cheese, 1 teaspoon dry mustard, and 1 cup sour cream. Then add the milk/butter/Gruyère stuff and stir it all up together and crumble up all the bacon in it, too. Turn the pot on low for about 3 hours—you can use that time to set your affairs in order, write your will, lay out your burial clothes, etc. Then eat up! I'm so proud of Alexis, I could just weep.

Suculentos Platos de Carne de Vacuno de Mi Próximo Marido (Succulent Beef Dish of My Next Husband)

If The Cutest Boy in the World ever runs off with a blackjack dealer, I've got my next husband all picked out. His name is Robert St. John and he is THE most wonderful and adorable chef—and he has created, in my opinion, THE WORLD'S BEST POT ROAST, resulting in my falling hopelessly in love with him, or at least his pot roast. He does himself currently HAVE a wife, whom he seems excessively fond of—so that could be problematic, but I'll worry about that later, right now I'm pretty focused on his pot roast. (However, regarding that Mrs., it's handy that her name is also JILL—so I think it will be a plus for him that he won't have to learn a new name. He'll just have to adjust to "Jill" being a big hungry hulk instead of a really cute blonde. I'm sure with time, he'll adjust.) You might think me shallow for being willing to marry a man for a tasty pot roast. Trust me, I've done a lot more for a lot less.

Robert's original recipe is in one of his MANY outstanding cookbooks—*DEEP SOUTH STAPLES: or How to Survive in a Southern Kitchen without a Can of Cream of Mushroom Soup*—I am giving it to you here with the slight modifications that I have made to it on account of he cooks his in an actual oven and I cook mine—you know—in my CROCK-POT®—because I just loooove my Crock-Pot®. I swear, it's like somebody else cooked—you just come home and a miracle has happened in your kitchen. I love it!

Anyway, the recipe calls for a 2½- to 3-pound shoulder roast. I have found that I can do TWO in my big-ass Crock-Pot® at the SAME TIME—which either serves a crowd OR (my favorite thing) makes for MASSIVE leftovers. Whether you do one or two roasts, the rest of the recipe is the same—you don't have to double anything—it makes a boatload of gravy with just the single recipe's ingredients.

·   ·   ·

HERE'S ALL YOU do: Heat ¼ cup of either bacon grease or canola oil in a heavy skillet. Season the roast(s) with kosher salt, black pepper, and Robert's own Steak Seasoning (available at rob ertsjohn.com). (I have a sensitivity to black pepper—so all I use is the kosher salt, garlic powder, and onion powder.) Brown the roast(s) on all sides and put them in the Crock-Pot®.

Then lower the heat on the skillet and put in ¼ cup olive oil and ½ cup flour—to make a peanut butter–colored roux. Add 2 cups diced onion (I just use a bag of frozen chopped onions—works perfectly) and ¼ teaspoon thyme, and cook for about 4 to 5 minutes. Then add 3 cups hot beef broth, 2 teaspoons Worcestershire sauce, 1 teaspoon salt, and 1 teaspoon black pepper. (I don't use the pepper.) Stir all that until it's smooth (except for the onion bits, obviously) and pour it over the roast(s). Cook it on low for 10 hours or so.

After it's been cooking just a very short time, the house will smell so good, you will think you will DIE if you don't get to eat that sucker NOW. By the time it's done, everyone will be WEEP-ING with anticipation—and then joy at first bite. I will eat this, gravy and all, completely cold out of the refrigerator the next morning, too. It's THAT good.

My Next Husband's Grilled Sweet Potatoes

In yet ANOTHER of my next husband's outstanding cook-books, this one entitled *New South Grilling* (see the link to all things Robert St. John on my FRIENDS page at www.sweetpo tatoqueens.com), he has come up with a most Queenly Sweet Potato recipe. I'm going to try to get him to come to the Parade and cook some for us. He has applied for Spud Studship and we have granted him an Apprenticeship, and we have also asked his Jill to join us as an O-fficial Wannabe. Their first duty in our service will be to feed us—pretty slick, huh?

• • •

FIRST, YOU PEEL 4 sweet potatoes and cut them into ½-inch slices. Mix together ½ cup soft unsalted butter, 2 tablespoons dark brown sugar, ¼ teaspoon cinnamon, and 1 teaspoon hot sauce. (Robert makes some EXCELLENT hot sauces—I use only his.) Put the tater slices on a cookie sheet and brush them with the butter stuff. Then put them on the grill (direct medium heat), buttered side down. Brush the tops with more butter and cook them for 12 to 15 minutes, turning once during that time. When they are fork-tender, take them off the grill, brush any remaining butter on them, and sprinkle them with kosher salt and black pepper (if you like it).

If there are any additional diners—other than yourownself, I mean—you prolly shoulda cooked more than 4. You'll have eaten those before you get them to the table.

Martha Jean's By-Gawd Apple Enchiladas

Martha Jean is from Booneville, Mississippi, and that puts her several cuts above just about everybody—especially anybody from, say, Guntown or Baldwyn. She also loves Jesus, though she does take a drink—now and then—which when you actually think about it means ALL THE TIME, and that's just not so. Booneville is not, after all, the Delta. Martha Jean is a By-Gawd Southern Cook, and many of us in the Queendom have been the regular recipients of her famous jams and jellies. Her friend Robin also brought me some jelly once—not only was it not ho-made, it was not even a name brand—I still have it, naturally—it was a GIFT, after all, and I think of Robin every time I see that discount-store jar of grape jelly.

Here is a dessert Martha Jean was known for—until she

went off and joined the Pilates Cult and became a stick. We are praying for her deprogramming.

.   .   .

TAKE ABOUT 6 to 8 flour tortillas and roll them up with some apple pie filling. Put them in a baking pan, seam side down, and sprinkle them with a bunch of cinnamon. Melt together ½ cup butter, ½ cup sugar, ½ cup dark brown sugar, and ½ cup water. Bring that to a boil and then let it simmer for about 3 minutes, then pour it over your enchiladas and let it sit for about 30 minutes. Then bake it at 350°F for about 20 minutes and serve immediately with 'niller ice cream.

When Martha Jean gets rescued from the Pilates, maybe we can get her to make us some. It's what we're living for.

All the Good Cooks Have Moved to West Point, Georgia

As I mentioned elsewhere in this book, I have been to West Point, Georgia, several times and I intend to go back—soon and often—and I recommend you put it on your travel list as well—for the FOOD. When you get to town, go directly to the Heart of the South Tea Room and get you some fried black-eyed peas on account of you cannot get them anyplace else—ON EARTH—and that right there is reason enough to go. It's fun to eat them and try to figure out how the hell they make 'em—and trust me, they will NOT tell you!

If you're an author, get the local library to have a book signing for you because the whole town will come and they will bring food for days. This has become my favorite stop on my book tour for obvious reasons.

You might get some of MICHAEL'S MAGICAL SWEET POTATO MUFFINS, but in case you don't rate that high (boo-hoo for you!)—here's how to make 'em:

Michael's Magical Sweet Potato Muffins

WHISK TOGETHER 1 cup dark brown sugar, ½ cup oil, 1 running-over teaspoon vanilla, and 2 eggs. Then, in another bowl, mix together 2 cups all-purpose flour, 2 teaspoons baking powder, 1 teaspoon cinnamon, 1 teaspoon nutmeg, ½ teaspoon allspice, and ½ teaspoon salt. To that, add 2 big giant sweet potatoes— either baked or boiled—and mashed. I suppose you COULD use canned ones, but it kinda makes me gag to think about. Add your egg/sugar mixture to all of that and stir it up without beating it to death. Put it in greased muffin tins and bake for about 25 to 30 minutes at 350°F. (If you want to, you could add ½ cup raisins or 1 cup pecans. I'd go with the pecans—not a big fan of raisins in stuff, but that's just me.)

Okay—I have got two pieces of life-altering good news for you now. First, I am gonna tell you how to make TEXAS CORN-

BREAD, which you may or may not thank me for in the long run on account of it is addictive and you may be the SIZE of Texas before too long. I do not know WHY it is called Texas Cornbread—there is no cornmeal in it—it has nothing to do with cornbread as we know it—but that is what Miss Red, granny of Queen LuAnne Berlin, called it, and we are not about to start arguing with Miss Red. We are too busy adoring her. (Note: This is, and will probably remain, the ONLY recipe I have EVER endorsed that actually contains LIGHT brown sugar. You KNOW how I feel about it from earlier books, and thus, you KNOW just HOW good this must BE—for me to be willing to use the stuff.)

Texas Cornbread

MIX ALL THIS in a bowl: 1 cup plain flour, 1 cup self-rising flour, 1 packed cup LIGHT brown sugar (yuck, but trust me), 1 cup white sugar, 4 eggs, 1 cup vegetable oil, 2 cups chopped pecans, and 1 running-over teaspoon vanilla. Put it into a greased 10 by 14-inch pan—the size of the pan matters—I bought this size especially for this recipe. Bake at 350°F for about 20 to 25 minutes, then rotate the pan and bake it for a few more minutes.

The baking time is tricky and important so watch it closely. Your oven may have it done in 20 minutes—in which case, skip the turning and additional oven time. I cook mine for 20 minutes exactly. You want it to be kinda chewy, so you don't want to overcook it. It is GOOD even if it is overcooked—there still won't be any leftovers—but when it's chewy, whoo-lard! You just can't believe how good it is. And it's real sneaky. You take the first bite and you just kinda acknowledge that it's pleasant-tasting—but then it sorta wakes up something on your tongue and you get that second bite, and from then on you're like a bed of bream on a bucket of crickets—just thrashing around, trying to get more and eating it as fast as you can, and you can't quit until it's gone.

The OTHER thing I'm gonna share with you is the GREAT GOOD NEWS that you can ORDER Texas Cornbread and a whole big pile of other YUMMY STUFF—and have it SHIPPED DIRECTLY TO YOU by Queen LuAnne and her Spud Stud, Craig. Unfortunately, Miss Red has passed on—but luckily she entrusted LuAnne with all her recipes, so Miss Red's Place—and we—are saved. LuAnne allows as how she has THE CUTEST FEDEX GUY EVER and so she hopes you order lots and often.

I don't know how they do it—the prices are UNBELIEV-ABLE—so order a bunch right away before they figger out they are practically GIVING THIS STUFF AWAY! I'm telling you, a GALLON of lobster bisque is $26—sausage balls are 60 for $16—TWO of Craig's Favorite Meatloaves are $22. Log on to www.missredsplace.com and Lu will send you a full menu. You may never cook for yourself again—at these prices, why would you?!

22

After Fifty

I've seen that written, I've heard it said, I've seen it happen to others, and believe me, I've experienced it in assorted very personal ways. It sucks.

I could just say "The End," I suppose, and that would sum it up for some folks. But those are the folks who were more than likely F-F-F-F-F-T after FIFTEEN. They were joyless then, have been joyless ever since, and will remain joyless until they finally do just fizzle completely on out, like the fuse on a dud firecracker.

For those of us who prefer to think of all that f-f-f-f-f-ing as our SIZZLING sound—building ever hotter and higher, right up to our last big crashing KA-POW!—well, let's take a look at some of those *f*'s.

Faith. This is a big one for me. I recommend it to you highly. I know people with lots—know people with none. In my observation and experience, shit happens to everybody. The faithful aren't immune but they sure do seem to fare better. It's not what happens to us in our lives that determines who and what we are—it's the choices we make about how to deal with it that forms our character.

Frying. No, I don't think it's second in importance only to faith—I just thought it would be funny to put it there. Funny is important to me, too. Not that frying is UNIMPORTANT to me—I am fairly fond—perhaps foolishly so—of flavorful fried foods. But frequently frequenting fabulous fried feasts will mean farewell forever to foxy fashions and finery and finally force us to face famine in order to fight the fat.

Family. We don't get to choose the families we're born into. Some of us are incredibly lucky with this—some of us are real-life Waltons. Some of us had childhoods that seemed like never-ending nightmares. But they did end. No matter how bad your childhood may have been—IT IS OVER and what you do with the REST of your life is totally up to you.

Faith. Family. Friends. Failure. Forgiveness.

We all fail from time to time. We fail at school, we fail at work, we fail our friends and families in countless ways, big and small. There is just so much to learn in life. And it's like taking

tests in school—often you don't really know if you learned anything or not until the test is over, and sometimes then it is too
late to get credit for the course.

Relationships are like that, I think. You go along with this
person or that and you think you're understanding it—all seems
well until there is a big test—a pop quiz—and you didn't know
it was coming and you sure didn't know it was gonna count for
99 percent of your grade—and before you know what hit you,
you have flat failed the class.

Failing AT something—anything—does NOT make YOU a
failure. God made you and He made you just the way He intended to make you and He doesn't make any trash. Whatever
happens to us, no matter what we do—That Person—who
God made—is still right there and it is never too late for That
Person.

The good news is that we can start over anytime, at any moment, and choose to do something different, something better.
This won't erase the pain our failure caused us or others, but it
does make way for forgiveness in the future. What the world
needs now—besides love, sweet love—is a whole big lot of forgiveness.

Forgive it—whatever it is—forgive it—and forget it—hold
fast to the lesson you learned from the pain, lest you repeat
your mistake—but forget the pain. Forgive others—even if they
don't forgive you. Forgive yourself—even if others don't forgive
you. Their lack of forgiveness says much more about them than

it does about you, and by the way, it's not your problem or your business.

A word about getting fired—that's a really scary *f*, and usually our first reaction to it is fear and a sense of failure—more bad *f*'s. But I believe, and it has been my own experience, that what it really is offering us is a chance to move forward—if we will just LOOK for the opportunity. We are finally free of what was a bad situation—and something fabulous is just waiting for us.

When my daughter was little bitty, I was divorced, left heavily in debt by someone else's unquenchable desire for cashmere socks and racing tires, taking care of my sick mother, working full-time as a personal trainer, and writing for three different newspapers—just to keep our heads slightly above the rising water—when, with no warning, one of the papers dropped my story—because the new editor felt that I was "not funny." I freaked.

I was not only out the money that I very desperately needed—but I was insulted on a very personal and vulnerable level. Writing was one of the very few things I believed I was actually good at—and this guy not only felt otherwise, he felt it strongly enough to flat-out FIRE me, with no warning or chance to change to suit him.

Fortunately, I needed the money badly enough that I did not have the time to indulge myself in the luxury of self-pity—I had to get off my ass and find a way to replace that three hundred dollars a month—or the home fires would be fizzling out very soon. That was the ONLY reason I EVER pursued a book deal. Had I not been fired, I would have continued working four jobs—and just been happy that the ends were meeting.

That pretty much covers the *f*'s—and do take note of the one Big *F* I am intentionally leaving out because this is a Serious Moment, but just for the record, I hope you do a lot of it, in a very loving way, on account of it's good for your complexion and it's especially good for your disposition, and that helps everybody, doesn't it?—so do it for yourself, your partner, your community, your country, and the world!

And that leaves us with the one, solitary *t* at the end of our "f-f-f-f-f-t." What's that *t* for? Could be for *trouble.* You get to decide if you want to HAVE trouble—or if you want to BE trouble, and I mean that in a good way, of course. Somebody sent me this the other day and I love it—I've looked for the person who originated it, but so far nobody's claiming credit: "Live life in such a way that every morning when your feet hit the floor, the Devil says, "OH, SHIT! SHE'S UP!"

We have a T-shirt on our Web site that says, "LIVE EVERY DAY LIKE YOU'VE GOT ALL DAY TOMORROW TO APOLOGIZE!" And by that, I'm not endorsing irresponsible and/or inconsiderate behavior. What I want you to do is HAVE SOME FUN. Failure to Frolic is a major cause of regret later in life; so, if you're behind on it, CATCH UP.

Tantalize is a most excellent *t* word. What a delight it is to be tantalized by something—anything—new shoes, big wads of chocolate, your lover. Possibly even more delightful to BE tantalizing, huh? Take time to tantalize today!

And I think that's what the *t* has got to be for: it's for TODAY—because no matter who you are, no matter what you are, whatever your faith or lack thereof—TODAY is all there is, for any of us.

I recently heard Amy Grant speak—and it was every bit as moving as hearing her sing, which is saying a lot. She said that she had tried over the years, with all good intentions, to set aside daily time for devotional reading and study. She had amassed all manner of books and tapes and whatnot for this purpose but they just gathered dust as the TIME just never seemed to make itself available.

Then she was struck by one verse in her Bible—Psalm 118:24—"This is the day that the Lord hath made, let us rejoice and be glad in it." And she found her daily devotional. She goes outside with her morning coffee, and in the still quiet, she looks around and says the verse over and over, varying the emphasis each time—THIS is the day, This IS the day, This is THE day, etc.

Please take note that the verse says "THIS" is the day—meaning TODAY—the one we are in right now—it does NOT say "YESTERDAY" was the day—although He did make it but it no longer matters because it is O-VER. It does not say "TOMORROW" is the day—although, if tomorrow does, in fact, show up, it will be because the Lord made it, too—but so far He has not committed to it so that's a crapshoot—TODAY is what we got—it is ALL that we've got and it is enough. Be Thankful for it—another *t* word worthy of note—and Trust (yet another one) that whatever you need will be there for you.

No matter what you put your faith in—from AA to Zen—you will find that you are called, exhorted, encouraged, and/or commanded to BE HERE NOW. So now I'm telling you that as well: you are FABULOUS, just as you are, right NOW, and you HAVE this wonderful day—so go freely forth, have fun—IT IS TOO LATE TO HAVE A BETTER PAST—what you do TODAY is all that matters. Then, if it turns out that you DO get a tomorrow, if you've done a bunch of good stuff TODAY, you will have created a new and better past for yourself, if you're still determined to dwell on it.

F-F-F-F-F-T AFTER FIFTY—FINE BY ME! I am from the generation that decreed "NEVER TRUST ANYBODY OVER THIRTY." When we said that, it sounded so cool and sophisticated—imagine our surprise when we found OURSELVES in that untrustworthy group. Over the past few decades, we have seen the error of our ways, we do heartily repent, and now we have THIS to say: "NEVER TRUST ANYBODY OVER EIGHTY-FIVE!"